THE COMPLETE ENOCHIAN DICTIONARY

DR. JOHN DEE

EDWARD KELLEY

THE COMPLETE ENOCHIAN DICTIONARY

A Dictionary of the *Angelic Language as Revealed to Dr. John Dee & Edward Kelley*

DONALD C. LAYCOCK

Preface by STEPHEN SKINNER
Foreword by LON MILO DUQUETTE

WEISER BOOKS

This edition first published in 2023 by Weiser Books, an imprint of
Red Wheel/Weiser, LLC
With offices at:
65 Parker Street, Suite 7
Newburyport, MA 01950
www.redwheelweiser.com

ISBN: 978-1-57863-796-6
Library of Congress Control Number: 2023930507

Cover design by Sky Peck Design
Cover art by Cameraphoto Arte Venezia / Bridgeman Images

Printed in the United States of America
IBI
10 9 8 7 6 5 4 3 2 1

CONTENTS

FOREWORD

by Lon Milo DuQuette

His life is a watch or a vision
Between a sleep and a sleep.
—Algernon Swinburne,
Atalanta in Calydon

An eternal debate rages between those who believe in the objective existence of spiritual entities, and those who believe that all such phenomena, no matter how apparently substantial, are entirely subjective experiences. Perhaps both schools of thought are correct. Where angels, demons, and spirits are concerned, I personally believe *it's all in your head—you just have no idea how big your head is.* Or, to quote my pseudepigraphic guru, Rabbi Lamed Ben Clifford, "Yes, the spirits are real. Yes, the spirits are imaginary. Most of us, however, cannot imagine how real our imaginations are."

I can, with no small measure of confidence, generally defend this position with jabs of well-worn qabalistic suppositions concerning the nature of consciousness and the functions of the various parts of the soul, and a left hook from Carl Jung. There have been times, however, when my field theory has been mightily challenged. Mr. Laycock's *Complete Enochian Dictionary* played a curious role in one such magical bout.

In 1978, as part of my perceived duties as an O.T.O.[1] lodgemaster, I began what would become a 23-year weekly magick class at my home in Costa Mesa, California. At the time, I was hard-pressed to stay one jump ahead of the enthusiastic aspirants who crowded my living room floor each Thursday evening. Within a year or so I realized that if I intended to continue teaching, I had learn more myself.

My magick library was pitifully small in those days. My newest treasure was a first edition of *Gems from the Equinox,*[2] which contains a selection of books, articles, essays, and rituals from Aleister Crowley's monumental work, *The Equinox.*[3] I combed through it to see if I could find something novel and exotic to occupy our Thursday nights for a while. I settled on *Liber LXXXIV, vel Chanokh—A Brief Abstract of the Symbolic Representation of the Universe Derived by Dr. John Dee Through the Skrying of Sir Edward Kelly.* It is Crowley's introduction to the complex and beautiful magical art form that has come to be known as Enochian. I didn't know it at the time, but *Chanokh,* and the book you are now holding in your hands, would dramatically change the course of my life.

At first I found *Chanokh* completely unfathomable. I read it, re-read it, and checked it against the Enochian material in Regardie's *Golden Dawn.*[4] After a day or two of whimpering, I finally started to see the light. The material that treated upon the evocation of angels of the four Elemental Tablets appeared to be the logical place to start the class.

Each Elemental Tablet is made up of 156 lettered squares, each of which is divided so to represent a truncated pyramid. Each has its own particular mixture of elements determined by a most impressive application of Hermetic logic. An angel (whose name is the letter of the square) "lives" in every one of the pyramids. These single-letter-named angels are modular and join with their neighbors to form bigger angels with longer names and more complex attributes and duties. It is truly an elegant system.

My plan was to keep the class occupied for a few weeks by having them draw and color their own tablets while I consulted with Dr. Regardie and constructed a set of three-dimensional tablets. Regardie was not keen on the idea. He told me that, to his knowledge, no one had ever done such a thing before, and that the Enochian angels were dangerous enough when they inhabited flat tablets. He cautioned, "Don't give them dimensional elbow-room." I joked, and suggested that *his* angels were probably in a bad mood because they were all squished up inside his flat tablets. I went ahead and prevailed upon a lodge brother to cut 624 wooden truncated pyramids.

These I would eventually prepare, paint, and assemble into the 4 Elemental Tablets (one each for Fire, Water, Air, Earth).

The night of our first evocation arrived. I prepared our living room temple for the evocation of Laidrom, the Mars Senior of the Tablet of Earth.[5] The temple opening and operating procedures are outlined admirably in *Chanokh,* so there was very little to do but follow directions. I smugly congratulated myself on being so well prepared. What I wasn't prepared for, however, was the possibility that the evocation might actually work.

The first student to arrive was D. R., who proudly handed me his newly acquired first edition of Laycock's *The Complete Enochian Dictionary*—the first one I had ever seen.[6] As I always do when someone hands me something rare or expensive, I feigned profound gratitude and gushed, "Oh! Thank you!" He quickly snatched it back out of my hands.

Once the rest of the class arrived, I asked for a volunteer to read the Call in the angelic language and sit in the visionary driver's seat. To my great anxiety, our only volunteer was David Wilson, the most cynical member of the class. I was certain that our class curmudgeon would receive no vision whatsoever and all of our efforts would be the target of his ridicule for many months to come. Still, he was willing to give it a try, so I switched on our little tape recorder and we proceeded.

After I banished and opened the temple, David read the Call twice, closed his eyes, and sat quietly for only a few seconds. Then, to all of our surprise, he casually started to describe in great detail his vision of a desert of white crystalline sand that sprouted columns of volcanic rock.

We were all thrilled. I asked if he saw any living things, an angel, or a spirit. He said "No." I encouraged him to repeat the Call a third time. As soon as he was finished, he excitedly described an enormous black cone arising from beneath the sand. David fell silent for a moment. He told us the cone was opening. Then, with a shout that startled us all… "It's him! It's him! I see him!"

He described a large, humanoid figure seemingly constructed from the same material as the cone. It had no face, its head was egg-shaped and flat in front. Its fingerless hands had the appearance of mittens. "This is Laidrom!" David announced reverently.

We were all in shock. None of us were prepared for this. David reached for a pad of paper and a pencil and scribbled down a few notes and a sketch. Before I could stutter out words of welcome, David let out a nervous giggle and said,

"Lon, I feel like… I feel… I could make strange sounds."

"Go with it!" I don't think I really meant it.

"Naw-n tahelo hoh athayzo raygayef… this is…"

"No! Relax, let it happen!" I tried to sound calm.

"I mean it, I feel like and idiot. I'm too… *sil-si anxilxi-to-da-arp nan-ta (inaudible) … ef… efe thar-zi.* I'm sorry… that's all. Nothing like this has ever happened before. I just felt like doing it."

I didn't know what to say. I finally salvaged the presence of mind to thank Laidrom for appearing. I was painfully embarrassed that I couldn't think of anything to say to this perfectly well-mannered angel standing in my living room. I finally stuttered something stupid to the effect that we really appreciated him stopping by, and we'd sure like to visit with him again sometime soon, then I hurriedly closed and banished the temple.

For a few seconds no one said a word. Then everyone started talking at once. I rewound the tape and we listened to the strange words that had tumbled out of David's mouth. Of course they didn't make any sense, but it was such a thrill to hear them.

We rewound the tape repeatedly and eventually transcribed three audible strings of syllables:

naw-n tahelo hoh athayzo raygayeff

zil-zi-anzilzi-lo-da-arp nan-ta (inaudible)

ef...efee thar-zi.

We referred to D.R.'s *The Complete Enochian Dictionary*, and in short order discovered:

Nanta, elo Hoath zorge ef.

"Spirit of Earth, first worshiper friendly visit."

Zil zien

"stretch forth hands"

Zilodarp Nanta

"stretch forth and conquer Spirit of Earth"

Ef etharzi

"visit in peace."

David appeared uncharacteristically shaken by what had happened. He insisted, and I didn't doubt his truthfulness, that he had not so much as even glanced at any of the Enochian Calls before that evening.

For the next three years, we would hold class two nights a week and focus exclusively on Enochian magick. We would depend increasingly on *The Complete Enochian Dictionary* to help us navigate the complexities of the angelic hierarchies and serve as our pronunciation guide to angelic language. David's visions would continue to take us on amazing excursions to the Elemental worlds, but as he became more accustomed to hearing the words of the Calls, his talent for breaking spontaneously into the angelic tongue diminished and finally ceased altogether. Yet he remains the most talented seer I have ever encountered.

D. R., bless his heart, eventually moved away. We haven't heard from him in many years. I am forever grateful to him for bringing *The Complete Enochian Dictionary* to class that memorable night so many years ago. As you have probably guessed, I never returned it to him.

—Lon Milo DuQuette
Costa Mesa, California, 2001

---

1 Ordo Templi Orientis.

2 Israel Regardie, ed., *Gems from the Equinox, Instructions by Aleister Crowley for His Own Magical Order* (Scottsdale, AZ: New Falcon Publications, 1992).

3 Aleister Crowley, et al., *The Equinox Volume 1, Numbers 1-10* (York Beach, ME: Samuel Weiser, Inc., 1998).

4 Israel Regardie, ed., *The Golden Dawn* (St. Paul: Llewellyn Publications, 1992).

5 Each Elemental Tablet has a Solar King and six Planetary Seniors. These seven spirits are very high on the Enochian hierarchical ladder.

6 *The Complete Enochian Dictionary* was first published in London by Askin Publishers, LTD. in 1978.

Incomprehensibilis est in aeternitate tua

– the Angel Raphael to John Dee, 31 March 1583

PREFACE
TO THE THIRD EDITION

The republication of *The Complete Enochian Dictionary* almost three decades after I wrote the original preface is a significant milestone. In the intervening period, more than a dozen books on Dr. John Dee and the Enochian language have appeared. Some of these have advanced our knowledge of Dee and his magical systems by publishing more of his original works. Very few of these have added to our knowledge of Enochian, the language, and very few changes have needed to be made to this dictionary.

What is for certain is that there is a new generation of readers and practitioners (often very different classes of people) who are enthralled by the marvelous and detailed works of the good Doctor and his rather shifty skryer, Edward Kelley.

The first editon of this dictionary was published in the United Kingdom by Askin Publishers, a company no longer active. Askin published worthwhile texts and grimoires of the Western Magical Tradition which were not otherwise easily available to practitioners. Dr. Meric Casaubon's *True and Faithful Relation of What Passed for Many Yeers* [sic] *between Dr. John Dee and Some Spirits*, 1659—which was the first extensively printed source of Dee's magical actions, and which was first reprinted by Askin in 1974—has been subsequently reprinted at least twice more, demonstrating the perennial interest in Dee's works.

Don Laycock, my co-worker and friend in these Enochian mysteries, died on December 28, 1988. Don, as a Doctor of Linguistics at the University of Canberra, left behind many monuments to his work with language, including that of the Australian Aborigine and dialects and languages of the South Pacific. But of all these languages, none was so strange—or fascinated him as much—as the language of the angels, John Dee's Enochian.

During the year or so that he was in London, we spent many months in the British Museum, reading, copying and summarizing the original manuscripts. On some evenings, we worked together on the practical side of the invocations, and Don knew many of the Calls fluently and resoundingly by heart. For a while, a copy of the *Complete Enochian Dictionary* stood in the Manuscript Room of the British Museum as a reference aid to the decipherment of the original manuscripts themselves, until one unscrupulous scholar decided that he had more need of it than all the other readers!

The foundation of the British Museum's collection was the original collection of Sir Hans Sloane's rare books, manuscripts, and curiosities that were purchased by the trustees of the British Museum for 20,000 pounds in 1753. Among these manuscripts were John Dee's originals and Elias Ashmole's manuscript copies. In 1759, the British Museum was formally opened, and the present building was complete in 1847. The great reading room was opened ten years later. Dee certainly would have approved of his works finishing up there, as he had tried to interest Queen Elizabeth I in founding such a national book collection.

There are several distinct systems of magic in Dee's manuscripts. What Don and I discovered about his systems and his angels, both in the Museum and in the practical use of the Calls, was that they work, as Aleister Crowley subsequently discovered at Bou Saâda in the Algerian desert.

After the Elizabethan period there were other examples of both communication with the angels through mediums, and of great gullibility. An example of both of these occurs in *Goodwin Wharton* by Kent Clark (OUP, 1984) which is a summary of Wharton's diaries kept during his extraordinary life from 1653 to 1701. Wharton thought that he regularly conversed with the fairies, even the Faery Queen herself, and the angels, but each time in English. Don's work stands alone as a grammatical guide to the angelic language itself.

Like Dee, Wharton was interested in everything mechanical and spiritual, including practical deep sea diving (he invented several pieces of apparatus for this purpose), searching for treasure guarded by fierce spirits, and conversations with the angels (through his often pregnant skryer). Like Dee, Uriel was one of Wharton's favorite communicating angels. Wharton also had time for politics and had a permanent seat in the House of Commons, was involved in several royal intrigues, and was promoted from Lieutenant-Colonel of Cavalry to Lord of the Admiralty. A highly public life is not always incompatible with magical work, and a Renaissance tum of mind seems to have been a characteristic of such men. Some of Dee's non-magical works have appeared in modem scholarly editions, such as Wayne Shumaker's *John Dee on Modern Astronomy: Propaedeumata Aphoristica (1558 and 1568),* in Latin and English (University of California Press, 1978). Other Dee fragments from the *Monas Hieroglyphica* and his preface to Euclid, together with a sampling of his diaries were published by Gerald Suster in *John Dee Essential Readings* (Aquarian/Crucible, 1986).

Dee has appeared in at least two memorable fiction books. In the modern *The House of Dr. Dee,* by Peter Ackroyd (Hamish Hamilton, 1993), Dee is portrayed as living in a squalid tenement on Cloak Lane in Clerkenwell in East London, rather than in the historically correct rambling old house in Mortlake by the Thames in West London. Other considerable liberties were taken by the author who was interested in time shifts between Dee's time and the present. A much more magical portrayal of Dee appears in Gustav Meyrink's *The Angel of the West Window* (Daedalus, 1991), which involves the Emperor Rudolph of Prague, and some interesting Rosicrucian dreams and visions.

However, anyone wishing to really understand Dee's magical work—after the pious sentiments have been stripped out—had better look to the tradition of the early grimoires rather than to the later and more elaborate system which the Golden Dawn derived from Dee's work. Although the latter is very intellectually satisfying, the roots from which Enochian magic grew will be found in the rich compost of the grimoires, or grammars of sorcery which dealt with the calling of both angels and demons. Mathers, who helped build the Golden Dawn system, was also a great translator of grimoires, and if Aleister Crowley is to be believed, a great practitioner as well.

A classic example of such a grimoire is *The Sworn Book of Honorius the Magician, as composed by Honorius through counsel with the Angel Hocroell* (Heptangle Books, 1978) from two British Museum manuscripts by Daniel Driscoll. This was later re-edited by Joseph Peterson in *The Sworn Book of Honorius* (Ibis Press, 2016).

The seminal works that have been published in the last three decades, and which any serious student should acquire, apart from those listed in the bibliography, are:

Geoffrey James. *The Enochian Evocation of Dr. John* Dee (Heptangle Books, 1984);

Adam McLean. *A Treatise on Angel Magic, being a Complete translation of Ms. Harley 6482 in the British Library* (Phanes Press, 1990);

Joseph Peterson (editor). *John Dee's Five Books of Mystery: Original Sourcebook of Enochian Magic* (Weiser Books, 2003);

Robert Turner. *The Heptarchia Mystica of John Dee, a primer of hermetic science and magical procedure by the Elizabethan scholar-mage* (Aquarian Press, 1986);

———. *Elizabethan Magic* (Element Books, 1989).

The Enochian system is much more than just the books written about it. It is one of the more complex bridges ever built between this world and the world of daemons, spirits, and angels, a piece of spiritual engineering created by one of the most brilliant minds of his age. As such it deserves to be traversed with care, as it was filtered through the tricksy mind of Dee's mercurial skryer Edward Kelley.

Stephen Skinner
London 2022

PREFACE

During the 16th Century, Cracow, Antwerp and Prague were the great centres of magical and alchemical enquiry and experiment. Cornelius Agrippa published his *De Occulta Philosophia* in Antwerp in 1531. Prague during the reign of King Rudolf II was devoted to the Hermetic arts and sciences which fascinated its monarch to the exclusion of all else. King Stephen of Poland, who had his seat at Cracow, was related to the Hungarian Bathori family which legend identifies with Count Dracula. Together with Cracow, Prague inherited an extensive heritage of Hasidic Judaism with its heavy mystical, magical and qabalistic content, in fact it was in Prague in the 1580's that Rabbi Loew engendered the famous golem, a figure which has haunted the history of the practical qabalah, and the ghetto of Prague, ever since.

Dr John Dee (1527-1608), mathematician and Astrologer Royal to Queen Elizabeth I, author of the main introductory textbook on mathematics of his age and innovator of many of the navigational aids which enabled the Elizabethan explorers to discover the New World, visited each of these cities in turn. First Antwerp in 1550 (and later in 1562-4), then Cracow in 1584, where he had audience with Stephen Bathori (King of Poland and relative of Elizabeth Bathori, the 'Bloody Countess'), later passing through Hesse-Cassel (a centre of Rosicrucian activity) after visiting Prague and Trebona during 1586-9.

John Dee's interest in magic arose out of his comprehensive studies, typical of the Renaissance man of the time, which commenced with Latin, an essential requisite of any scholar of the period, at the age of ten. Five years later he was sent to Cambridge, where he studied the traditional *Trivium* of subjects, grammar, rhetoric and logic. However it was not till the following years when he undertook the *Quadrivium* (arithmetic, geometry, music and astronomy), that his studies, and the eventual direction of his life work really got underway, for as he says himself 'I was so vehemently bent to studie, that for those yeares I did inviolably keepe this order; only to sleepe four houres every night; to allow to meate and drink (and some refreshing after) two houres every day; and of the other eighteen houres all (except the time of going to and being at divine service) was spent in my studies and learning.'

At the same time he mastered the two *Tongues,* Greek and Hebrew (the latter not quite as thoroughly as the former) and the *Three Philosophies,* natural, moral and metaphysical.

In 1546 Dee's position as an under-reader in Greek and a founding fellow of Trinity College, Cambridge, seemed to promise the beginnings of a brilliant academic career, but the following summer he visited the Low Countries where his interest in geography flowered, following his acquaintance with Giraldus Mercator (the famous Dutch cartographer responsible for the well-known square-grid Mercator map projection), and Gemma Frisius, both of whom provided him with geographical equipment, globes, astronomer's staff and ring, and material on the art of navigation, which he duly took back to his university.

Having realised that some arts and sciences were very much further advanced in Europe than in England, and realising that England could profit by these, he visited Louvain the following summer. In 1550 a short trip to Antwerp brought him in contact with another geographer, Abraham Ortelius (whose house still stands in Antwerp, and whose detailed geographical charts and equipment now reside in the Antwerp Navigational Museum). Pursuing his other great interest, Mathematics, he lectured on Euclid in Paris, to packed halls, establishing his reputation immediately. He was offered a post of King's Reader in Mathematics at Paris University on a stipend of two hundred crowns, which for patriotic reasons Dee refused. This pattern was consistently repeated, with Dee refusing to quit the service of Elizabeth I for far more lucrative positions. On several occasions, the Czar of Russia, Fedor I, offered Dee a position in his court as advisor and physician, at the incredible salary of 2,000 crowns a year, with food supplied from the table of the Czar himself, and a house and additional salary from the Lord Protector, but the offer was again turned down by Dee. Returning to England the following year, he met Jerome Cardan (1552) who was probably responsible for stirring up Dee's interest in the mathematical conjuration of spirits and reinforcing the influences that Dee must most certainly have encountered earlier in his career at Antwerp.

These interests were almost nipped in the bud by the accession of Queen Mary to the throne, when his ambiguous interest in magic coupled with the implied heresy of his predominantly Protestant leanings resulted in his imprisonment for three months in 1555. Interestingly enough, his skill in theology resulted in Dee being requested by the Bishop of London to act as a judge in one of the heresy trials, in which he was one of the accused.

When Elizabeth I succeeded to the throne, John Dee's fortunes changed considerably: he was even asked to select (with due recourse to the influence of the stars) a propitious date for her coronation: a calculation which by all accounts of the Elizabethan era, must have been well performed!

Five years later Dee set out to visit various centres of learning making a very rapid tour of most of Europe including Antwerp, where he met Christopher Plantin (whose presses, which still exist, were justly famous throughout Europe, and whose type design provided the model for that used in setting this book). Here he secured a copy of Trithemius' influential *Steganographia* (concerned with 'angel-magic', and perhaps cryptography), before visiting Zurich, Urbino, Rome (where legend has it that he had audience with the Pope), Venice, and finally Presburg in Hungary where he was granted audience with Maximillian II, to whom he was later to dedicate his *Monas Hieroglyphica*.

Dee wrote the *Monas* in seven days in 1564, and in the same year it was published in Antwerp. Significantly it was not to appear in Dee's native tongue till 1947. The *Monas*, whose full title, *The Monad, Hieroglyphically, Mathematically, Magically, Cabbalistically and Anagogically Explained* gives a fair indication of its complexity and scope, is a unique blend of some of the more picturesque alchemical allegories woven into the otherwise rather dry fabric of a book, constructed as a series of exact Euclidean type theorems; with liberal sprinklings of interpretations of the Monas itself (which was a combination of the symbols for Mercury and Aries drawn in a specific proportion). This is elaborated with geometric details for drawing the Monas, and an explanation of the symbolic meanings of these proportions.

In the same year as the *Monas* was published, Dee went to live south-west of London, at Mortlake, in a rambling old house well-provided with various outhouses for his many scientific interests.

The site of the house, opposite the Church of St Mary the Virgin which Dee later endowed, and in which he is buried, abuts onto the Thames. Elizabeth I often came to visit him by Royal barge from Richmond or Hampton Court Palace.

From here, living on the income of several rectories, Dee quietly pursued his studies, which included writing a classic preface to the first English edition of *Euclid's Elements of Geometrie,* and planning voyages in search of the north-west passage, or for gold in Labrador. He reputedly accompanied Martin Frobisher on at least one of these exploratory voyages.

In response to Elizabeth's request to Dee for information about the lands to which she was heir, he wrote a work called *Of Famous and Rich Discoveries*. . ., which whilst purporting to be a treatise on various voyages of discovery undertaken by Europeans (later to be used by Hakluyt as a source for his accounts), was in fact designed to promote Elizabeth's Imperial aspirations, by assuring her of her rightful ownership of various lands, by appealing to historical precedent. Considering Dee's reputation, it is interesting that he was also called on by the Queen to counteract the effects of a wax image which had been discovered in Lincoln's Inn Fields, and which was thought to be part of a magical plot against her. This establishes Dee's court reputation as that of magician as as well as a geographer and mathematician.

After a first marriage which lasted just one year, he married Jane Fromond (a member of the Queen's household) and three years later took up what he considered to be the most important study of his life. This was the communication, via the medium of a *shewstone* with 'angels' in an attempt to quench his overmastering desire for knowledge beyond that normally accessible to mortals, to reach up in fact, like Enoch or the Biblical prophets, to God, the very source of knowledge itself. As Dee put it:

> 'I have often read in thy (God's) books and records, how Enoch injoyed thy favour and conversation; with Moses thou was familiar; And also that to Abraham, Isaack and Jacob, Joshua, Gideon, Esdras, Daniel, Tobias and sundry others thy good angels were sent by thy disposition, to Instruct them, informe them, helpe them, yea in worldly and domestick affaires, yea and sometymes

> to satisfie their desires, doubtes, and questions of thy Secrete: And furdermore considering, the Shewstone, which the High Prieste did use, by thy owne ordering... that this wisdome could not be come by at mans hand or by humaine power, but only from thee (ô God).'

Dee reasoned that intercourse with these 'spiritual creatures', provided that malevolent, misleading and demonic spirits were banished, was one of the highest ends man could aim at. It is here that magic enters Dee's work. The exactness of mathematics allied with the convoluted philosophy of the Hebrew qabalah and Arabic magico-alchemical works, produced a very solid base from which magic (both natural and metaphysical) could be approached in a scientific manner. This had two effects. First it attracted men of Dee's calibre to the study of magic. However the second effect of this union was the tarring of mathematics with the same brush as had previously been reserved for the heretic or the local practitioner of wort-cunning. This attitude resulted in the sack of Dee's house at Mortlake (during his absence in Europe) and the haphazard destruction of some of his scientific equipment. Ironically enough his 'instruments of sorcery', his skrying stones, Holy Table, wax tablets lamen and chest containing the *Libri Mysteriorum* accompanied him to the Continent, and so escaped the rage of the mob.

However it was in 1581, before Dee left for Europe, that he began his magical experiments. His avowed aim was to establish contact with the angels, to discover that knowledge which was not to be had either from books or from experiment.

During this period Dee employed Edward Kelley and several other *skryers,* or seers, to obtain a series of communications which he attributed to the agency of angels and spirits. Despite the fact that the first record of the skrying is dated December 22nd, there is evidence to suggest that the skrying began in a haphazard way as early as March 8th, 1581. The first workings were based on a grimoire type of approach, relying to an extent on equipment. This included wax tablets, a skrying table, a gold lamen and several shewstones, of obsidian and rock crystal. This was evolved into a sophisticated system which involved setting the skrying stone (several were used including a conventional looking crystal

The wax *Sigillum Emeth* used to support the skrying stone. (Courtesy of the Trustees of the British Museum).

ball and the black obsidian mirror) upon the elaborately engraved Sigillum Aemeth (still preserved in the British Museum) which was in turn placed upon a special table inscribed with a hexagram, enclosed within a frame of Enochian letters, and supporting seven specially designed talismans, the whole insulated from the floor by a further four wax tablets, miniature versions of the larger Sigillum Aemeth.

The early communications set down in Dee's *Libri Mysteriorum* deal with communications from Annael and Uriel, who dictated exact instructions for the engraving of the table, lamen, ring and sigils required. The third book opens with the designs for the seven talismans to be used on the skrying table, and concludes with the *Tabula Collecta* of the 49 angels whose invocatory modus operandi is explained in the fourth book.

Dee and Kelley pressed on, skrying now as often as several times a day till the complete outline of a self-contained system of magic was obtained and set down in Dee's manuscript, *De Heptarchia Mystica,* so named because of the 7×7 angels, whose invocations, hours, seals and sigils are described therein. Dee's description of two of these creatures will suffice to show their variety:

> 'He appeared in his red apparell: & he opened his Clothes & there did issue, mighty & most terrible gastly Flames of Fire out of his sides: which no mortall Eye could abide to looke upon any long while. And in the marvelous raging Fire, the word BRORGES did appeare tossed to and fro of the very flames. His Seale or Character is this . . .

And by way of contrast:

> 'Therefore he appeared in a long purple Gowne, & on his head a triple Crowne of Gold, with a measuring Rod of gold in his hand, divided into three equall parts: in the forme of a very well proportioned man.'

The significance of these descriptions is the light they throw on Dee's collection of 49 'Angelorum Bonorum', adding a Goetic dimension in much the same way that works like *The Sacred Magic of Abra-Melin the Mage* allows that it is as necessary for practitioners to exercise their authority over the evil or Qliphothic aspects, as it is over the more benevolent positive manifestations of the non-physical universe.

By March 1582, Kelley had commenced to transmit the first passages in the first version of that strange language Enochian. This material never found its way into print as has the better known later Enochian of the Calls which was made popular by the Hermetic Order of the Golden Dawn and later by Aleister Crowley. An example of this early Enochian, by way of contrast with the later (translated) material comes from an 'action' dated 5th April 1582:

> 'Amchama zeuoth luthimba ganeph iamda ox oho iephad mad noxa voscaph bamgephes noschol apeth iale lod ga NA zuma datques . . .'

Returning however to events in the external world, we find Dee correcting the Julian Calendar in 1582 to a greater degree of accuracy than any other contemporary mathematician (although the council of Archbishops turned down his proposals on the grounds that they smacked of Popishness, thereby putting off English calendar reform by several centuries).

In the same year Dee and Kelley met Count Albertus Laski, a palatine of Siradz and aspirant to the Polish Crown. The next year the Dee and Kelley household set out for Cracow.

It is at this stage that the published part of Dee's *Libri Mysteriorum* takes up the account. This was first printed from Dee's manuscript by Meric Casaubon in 1659 as *A True and Faithful Relation of what Passed for Many Yeers between Dr John Dee . . . and Some Spirits,* and re-issued by Askin Publishers, London, in 1974.

These 'angelic conversations' cover a wide range of material, from the enumeration of every country on the (then known) face of the earth with their presiding angels, through prophecy (of varying degreees of accuracy), to the amazing collection of transcripts in the Enochian tongue.

Amongst the more 'magical' material, despite passages of incredible triviality and banality, there is a hard core of extremely interesting material recurring throughout the 'angelic' conversations, such that Elias Ashmole (the famous antiquary and early Freemason), and later MacGregor Mathers, one of the founders of the Hermetic Order of the Golden Dawn, took portions of the system and derived from it their own systems of magic. Ashmole's attempts, covering a period of some five years (1671-76), are closer to the spirit of Dee's work than Mathers' interpretation, and tend to confirm the objectivity of the intelligences involved in the original communications.

Along these lines there is a record by a different experimenter dated 16th October, 1583, which tends to add weight to the objective existence of the phenomena recorded by Dee in *A True and Faithful Relation*... It begins:

> 'At ii a Clock at night, I & my Companions having begun Action, at the request & full consent of all the Company, we did fully agree, that we should not desist, till we had brought something to perfection, & having begun Action, & all things for the same purpose ready & fitted; thus give a briefe & true account of what followes.
>
> After the first Invocation, twice or thrice repeated, there appeared two Men, in the furthest Glass, visible to some part of the Company, & not to other some; but proceeding on, & Invocating highly, there came a very great blow upon the Floore, which made a very great noise, & before it ceased, it did whirle about severall tymes, to the astonishment & admiration of all ye Company, & still proceeding on, & reading further, there came something, which fell pat upon the Table, & from the Table upon the Ground, which made a smaller Noise upon ye floore, then the other did & so vanisht, & soe much for ye night, only when Action was ended, we could find nothing that was the cause of ye noise...'

Returning to a more modern application of Dee's work we find the brilliant syntheses by MacGregor Mathers into the syllabus of the Adeptus Minor grade of the Golden Dawn at the end of the 19th century. Although he used only a small part of the vast amount of material that Dee left, he incorporated the Elemental Tablets with their associated correspondences and the Thirty Calls of the Aethyrs before referred to, whilst Westcott, co-founder of the Order, elaborated a four-sided version of chess based on the Enochian system.

Much of Mathers' adaptation of the original system was done to make it compatible with the Golden Dawn's existing qabalistic basis, which, although ultimately based upon the qabalah that Dee was familiar with, contained many elements not found in Dee's original work, such as the Tarot Atus and the Egyptian Pantheon.

For Dee, the Angels also provided advice and reproof which he conveyed to two of the most powerful patrons he sought, Stephen Bathori King of Poland, and Rudolf II of Bohemia. He was lucky not to have incurred any more painful a punsihment for his pains than a partial banishment by the latter. Dee and Kelley accordingly sought refuge in 1586 at the castle of Count Rosenberg at Trebona, where Dee stayed for two years. Meanwhile Kelley managed, through his alchemical experiments, to curry favour first with the Count and then with Rudolf, who later knighted him.

A True and Faithful Relation... which opened in Lesden in May 1583 closes with the agreement between Dee and Kelley to 'hold their wives in common' (wife-swapping not being an entirely modern prerogative) at which point the whole tenor of the communications changes and passages of considerable power appear, contrary to anything Kelley had up to this point produced.

The spouse-swapping episode began with an alleged commandment by the Angels conveyed by Kelley, 'that we two had our two wives in such sort as we might use them in common' (April 18th, 1587). This was consummated on the night of 22nd May as is evident from semi-obliterated remarks in the original manuscript which were not printed by Casaubon.

This arrangement, which although productive of some of the most interesting material recorded by Dee, probably barely lasted till July 19th when Dee records ' a certayne kinde of recommendation between our wives. Next day saw relenting of E. K. also by my Lord's entrety'. Unfortunately with the exception of four pages in Casaubon these MS notes belong to the *greate Chasme* of 20 years from May 23, 1587 to March 20, 1607: the papers which fell into the hands of Elias Ashmole, but which do not appear to have survived. They contain Dee's record of the last 'actions' with Kelley before he left Dee's service.

The delivery of these passages is in many ways similar to several Gnostic works describing the descent of Sophia, *The Song of Solomon,* and Aleister Crowley's *Liber Legis,* with which there are some remarkable similarities in wording. Crowley, incidentally, claimed Edward Kelley as one of his past incarnations, which, rather than necessarily supporting transmigration of souls, suggests the affinity Crowley felt for Kelley's work, which may have led to a certain amount of unconscious plagiarism.

In February 1589 Dee saw the last of Kelley, and from thenceforth Dee's skrying experiments were with very inferior skryers such as Bartholomew Hickman, whose skrying records were later burnt when Dee discovered that he was a fraud. Till Kelley's death, Dee continued to hope for a reconciliation with his old skryer.

Dee's enthusiasm had not waned however for he named his next daughter Madimi, after the young girl who was a constant visitor to the crystal during the skrying sessions.

By this time he was back in his beloved England where he set about restoring his house in Mortlake which had been damaged by the mob during his six year absence. He partly re-assembled his collection of books which contained in excess of 2,500 books and manuscripts on mathematics, magic, alchemy, philosophy, cryptography, classical literature, geography and the qabalah.

The last six years of his life were spent under James I, an unpleasant situation for anybody remotely suspected of witchcraft, this monarch having been responsible for the most savage persecution of witches and magicians ever to occur in England.

Dee died in 1608 and was buried in the chancel of the church in Mortlake, opposite his house.

On one hand Dee is looked upon as a man of the Renaissance with heavy medieval leanings, rather like Elias Ashmole, who combined membership of the Royal Society (avowedly formed for the advancement of the empirical sciences) with intimate involvement in astrology, alchemy and other interests which would have been regarded as rather reactionary by other members of the Royal Society. On the other hand, the populace saw him as a sorcerer, or to use Dee's words when writing his own defence 'a companion of hellhounds, and a caller and conjurer of wicked and damned spirits'. Likewise Dee was regarded slightly askance at Court, although it seems he was never once doubted by Elizabeth I, to whom he remained devoted for the duration of his life. In between the rather dry but learned magus and the 'damned sorcerer' lies the real Dee: a man who perpetuated the tradition of Hermes Trismegistus and helped 'Christianize' the qabalah, who in all modesty aspired to be another Enoch, who wished to have God's word directly transmitted by God's messengers the angels, nevertheless a very humble man, as his many prayers preceding the skrying actions testify.

Dee is a very important link in the magical tradition, not only because he brought back ideas to England from European centres of learning, or because he aided the cross-fertilization of the Rosicrucian movement, as is aptly pointed out by Frances Yates in *The Rosicrucian Enlightenment,* but because his magical research is voluminous, carefully documented, and original.

Stephen Skinner
London 1975

INTRODUCTION TO THE THIRD EDITION

This dictionary is not a mere word list as were some of the other Enochian dictionaries produced over the last few decades. Instead it is a full and properly organised dictionary, with everything that conveys, assembled from the manuscript sources and written by a Professor of Linguistics.

Dr. Donald C Laycock (1936–1988) was an Australian linguist and anthropologist, usually remembered for his work on the languages of Papua New Guinea and the Pacific. Amongst his other claims to fame is his compilation of the first Dictionary of the Enochian language generated by the skrying of Sir Edward Kelley under the supervision of Dr. John Dee in the late 16th century.

Don was a graduate of the University of Newcastle, and later worked as a researcher in anthropology at the University of Adelaide. He undertook his Ph.D. at the Australian National University in linguistics and became a world authority on the languages of Papua New Guinea.

He made several pioneering surveys of the languages of the Sepik region of New Guinea. The first of these, his Ph.D. researched under the supervision of Stephen Wurm, was published as The Ndu Languages (1965), and this work established the existence of a closely related group of languages. In subsequent surveys, Laycock found the Ndu languages were part of an even larger language family extending through the middle and upper Sepik valley (which he referred to as the 'Sepik sub-phylum'). Later in 1973 he proposed that these languages formed part of a Sepik-Ramu phylum.

Laycock also first identified the Torricelli and Piawi groups of languages. He published numerous papers on the linguistics and anthropology of these New Guinea languages, hoping to document them before the advance of Western culture, especially the increasingly wide use of Pidgin English, wiped them from the memory of mankind.

He was described by his fellow authors of Skeptical (David Vernon, Dr. Colin Groves and Simon Brown) as a 20th-century renaissance man as his interests were wide-ranging from Melanesian languages, to magic, clairvoyance, Tarot cards, and bawdy songs.

He was a Fellow of the Australian Academy of the Humanities (FAHA), Vice President of the Australian Linguistic Society (ALS), and a member of Mensa. As a keen member of the Australian Skeptics, he entertained many people at Skeptics' conventions with his demonstrations of trance and glossolalia.

I met Don in London in the early 1970s, where we discovered we were both working on Dr John Dee's manuscripts in the Manuscript Reading room of the British Museum (later to become the British Library). We talked at length about these things and Don kindly asked me to dinner in the family home in North London where I met his wife Tanya and his children. At that time I had a verbal agreement with Israel Regardie to publish his version of an Enochian Dictionary, but after we examined it and realised that most of it was derived via Crowley, we instead decided to do a more complete Enochian Dictionary based directly on Dee's manuscripts, only adding Crowley's usage where it deviated from the original.

Don spent many diligent hours putting together every extant Enochian word and deciding its syntactic function, so that any Enochian passages, even corrupt ones, could be translated. He applied the same academic standards to producing this dictionary as he had to his other linguistic research into even more obscure languages. Don was a real Dee enthusiast, and together we met up with other researchers who had similar interests such as Vivian Godfrey and Leon Barcynski (aka Melita Denning and Osborne Phillips), two Masters of the Aurum Solis, who were both researching Dee and Enochian magic at the same time.

Don utilised the facilities of the huge but ageing Univac computer at the Australian National University in Canberra to analyse the language and determine if it was 'real' or made up by the ever-inventive Edward Kelley. Extraordinarily, the poor old card-fed Univac managed to break down almost every time it was fed the raw Enochian data.

In the days before word processing and computer-aided design, this book had to be hand set by Tom Graves, a friend who shared my interests in dowsing, stone circles, and the 'matter of Britain.'

After his death, Laycock's meticulous work on the Enochian language has survived and been an essential reference for anyone studying Dee's magic. He died, after a short illness, in Canberra, on 27 December 1988, just a year after this dictionary was first published by my company, Askin Publishers.

Stephen Skinner
London, January 2022

ENOCHIAN

Angelic language or mortal folly?

Languages come and languages go. Something like seven thousand natural languages have been recorded, in one form or another, since the beginning of recorded history; and at least a thousand more languages have been invented by men, for purposes ranging from magic to extraterrestrial communication.

But no language has a stranger history than the Enochian language documented in this dictionary. Perhaps strangest of all is that we still do not know whether it is a natural language or an invented language — or whether it is, perhaps, the language of the angels, as its originators believed. In this introduction, the data is presented for the reader to make up his own mind.

The personalities: John Dee (1527-1608)

According to the horoscope he later cast for himself, John Dee was born at Mortlake on the morning of 13 July, 1527, under the sign of Cancer, with Sagittarius in the ascendant — a good omen, say the astrologers, for a career based on learning and the occult. His father, Rowland Dee, was Superintendent of the Royal Table, at the English Court; but John Dee was later to claim a proud genealogy that included Welsh kings and princes, all the way back to King Arthur. Whatever the truth of these claims, it is certain that John Dee became a distinguished man in his own right. Though he published little, it is apparent that he exercised a powerful intellectual influence on the greatest minds of the time. He was a dedicated, even fanatical, scholar, resolving, when an undergraduate at Cambridge, to spend eighteen hours in study each day, with only four hours for sleep, and two hours for meals.

He graduated Master of Arts from Cambridge in 1548, and went abroad to study further at Louvain. Later he gave lectures at the University of Paris that attracted so many students that they had to crowd at the windows to listen: at this time, Dee was only twenty-three years old.

His reputation in Europe and at home continued to grow, though it was always tempered with the ignorant fear of him as a sorcerer and demonolator. He took few actual jobs, being dependent for most of his life on royal and ecclesiastical pensions —which never amounted to more than about eighty pounds a year. For most of his life, he was chronically short of money — which is not surprising when one takes into account that he spent more than three thousand pounds (or eighty thousand pounds in current value) on building up Elizabethan England's greatest library.

Some idea of the range of Dee's interests can be obtained from the contents of this library, which contained at least 2500 printed books and manuscripts. The works dealt with mathematics, alchemy, philosophy, classical literature, geography — and the hermetic tradition. Dee had thoroughly studied the 'Christian cabbala', particularly from the works of Cornelius Agrippa, and was to become more and more immersed in the qabalistic tradition as time went on.

In fact, Meric Casaubon, in his edition (1659) of part of the record of Dee's seances, scathingly described Dee as 'a Cabalistical man, up to the ears'. One can also get a good impression of Dee's character from this longer statement by Casaubon — although Casaubon himself does not think much of Dee's mind:

> 'Some men come into the world with *Cabalistical Brains;* their heads are full of mysteries; they see nothing, they read nothing, but their brain is on work to pick somewhat out of it that is not ordinary; and out of the very *A B C* that children are taught, rather than fail, they will fetch all the secrets of Gods Wisdom; tell you how the world was created, how governed, and what will be the end of all things. Reason and Sense that other men go by, they think the acorns that the old world fed upon; fools and children may be content with them but they see things by another *Light.*'

The description is a good one, but it can describe two kinds of individual: the magus, or the obsessed fool. Which Dee was, the reader will have to decide, on the basis of his spiritist seances. It is not known just when he began to seek or achieve effective communications with the beings he regarded as angels, but it was probably not before 1581. From about March of that year, as we learn from his *Private Diary*, he was troubled by odd dreams, and strange knockings in the night. To those who accept the objective reality of Dee's spirits, it would seem that the spirits were anxious to get in touch with him, rather than the other way round.

Be that as it may, by October of that year Dee had found a medium, one Barnabas Saul, who, using as a crystal a stone given Dee by a 'friend', reported to Dee the words of the angels Annael and Michael — and who later denied seeing any spirits at all, for fear of prosecution for conjuring. But Dee was dissatisfied with Saul as a medium, and dismissed him after working with him for only a few months.

The personalities: Edward Kelley (1555-1595)

Opportunely — for Dee's appetite for spiritual communications had been thoroughly whetted — there appeared at his house in Mortlake on 8 March 1582 a man calling himself Edward Talbot, afterwards to be known by his true name of Edward Kelley. Kelley was about twenty-seven years old at the time; but his previous life remains something of a mystery. There is a long-standing tradition — unfortunately not well-substantiated — that he had had his ears cut off for forgery. He seems to have been something of an occult charlatan, travelling England living off a reputation for alchemy and the preparation of magical elixirs. On several occasions he is known to have been in possession of old books, sometimes in cipher, purporting to give the location of buried treasures. He was not uneducated; he had been an undergraduate at Oxford, but was apparently dismissed. He spoke Latin well enough to travel in Europe, and converse with Dee's Continental friends; he makes frequent grammatical mistakes, but of his general intelligence there is no doubt.

Dee was at first suspicious of this young man who offered his services as a 'skryer', or mediumistic visionary; he seems to have thought that Kelley might have been a spy sent to gain information on his conjuring activities, to report him to the authorities. But the doubts must have been resolved, for already on 10 March that year Dee was giving the new medium a trial — with results so successful that there began on that day a strange and close association between the two men that was to last for some seven years, and to involve them in a series of actions with a host of spirits of

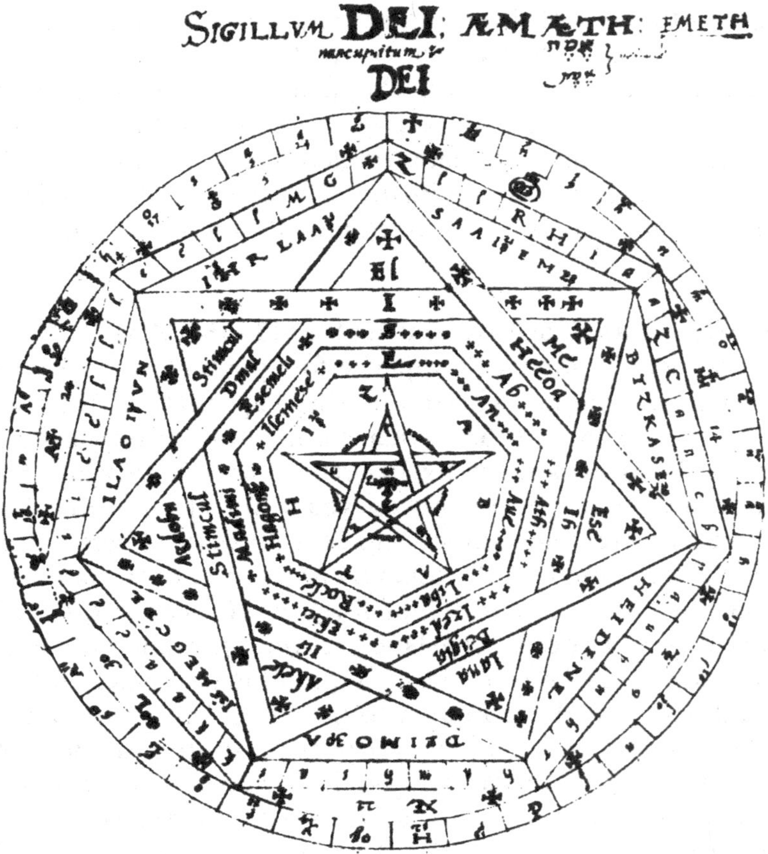

Dee's drawing of the *Sigillum Emeth* in Sloane MS 3188, f.30. (Courtesy of the British Library).

all ages and sexes, with magical tablets, lost and miraculously restored books, buried treasure, alchemical recipes, and in the end — a curiously modern touch — wife-swapping.

The first seances

Kelley was an immediate success as a medium, and on that first recorded occasion was granted a vision of Uriel, who revealed his secret sigil or signature, and gave the preliminary instructions for the construction of a powerful magical talisman, the Sigillum Emeth (or Aemeth), to be made of wax and used in further invocations. The original tablet, and smaller similar ones, can still be seen in the British Museum. The design may ultimately derive from Sloane manuscript 313; Kircher, in his book *Oedipus Aegyptiacus* (Rome, 1652-4), gives a version of the seal with traditional angelic names in place of the Enochian names of Dee. It is unlikely that he could have got this from Dee's manuscripts, then, as now, unpublished.

The pattern for almost all the recorded seances is established right at the beginning. The seance opens with a prayer, the magic crystal or 'shewstone' is uncovered, and Kelley sees visions and hears voices, whose content he transmits to Dee, the recorder. Several aids to scrying may have been used. Dee is usually credited with having at least two: a rock crystal globe, and a 'magic mirror' of black obsidian; both of these can be seen in the British Museum. Dee apparently saw and heard nothing (though this is arguable; his *Private Diary* entry for 25 May 1581 reads: 'Today I had sight offered me in chrystallo, and I saw', and at other times he seems to have heard at least some of the sounds produced, such as thunder, roaring and trumpets).

Many of Kelley's 'messages' consisted of letters of the alphabet arranged in squares. It will be necessary to examine some of the early examples in detail, if we are to be able to formulate any coherent theories about the mystical language that was produced at later sessions.

Two of the earliest squares transmitted by the 'spirits' through Kelley are the following:

Z	l	l	R	H	i	a
a	Z	C	a	a	c	b
p	a	u	p	n	h	r
h	d	m	h	i	a	i
k	k	a	a	e	e	e
i	i	e	e	l	l	l
e	e	l	l	M	G	†

[20 March 1582]

S	A	A	I^{21}_{8}	E	M	E^{8}
B	T	Z	K	A	S	E^{30}
H	E	I	D	E	N	E
D	E	I	M	O	30	A
I^{26}	M	E	G	C	B	E
I	L	A	O	I^{21}_{8}	V	N
I	H	R	L	A	A	$^{21}_{8}$

[21 March 1582]

With reference to the first square, Dee is instructed to 'read downward'; he does so, and, starting with the left-hand column, he finds the following angelic names: Zaphkiel, Zadekiel, Cumael, Raphael, Haniel, Michael, Gabriel (with the sign of the cross to fill up the last square).

The procedure with the second square is a bit more complicated. The numbers 8, 26 and 30 are to be read as 'L', at the end of names, 21 is the letter 'E'; and the names are to be read off diagonally, in a south-westerly direction, starting with the 'S' of the top left-hand corner. The following names are produced: (S)Zabathiel, Zedekie(i)l, Madimiel, Semeliel, Nogahel, Corabiel, Levanael.

Now, there is nothing new about most of these angelic names. Apart from the archangels Raphael, Michael and Gabriel (Uriel was dictating through Kelley at this point) most of the other names can be found, in identical or very similar forms, in standard magical texts such as those of Agrippa and Peter d'Abano — as Dee himself comments in a marginal note.

This being so, it is hard to believe that these angelic names are in any way *derived* from the squares; it seems much more likely that they are the *formants* of the squares. From such a square, once created, it is however possible to derive *new* names, and in fact Dee is presented with a series of names created from the second square, by reading in different directions along the diagonals. The names were dictated before the square itself was given; the vision was of seven men, seven women, seven 'wenches', and seven boys, each with letters on the fronts of their gowns. These 28 visionary manifestations are given planetary attributions, as follows:

Planet	*7 Women*	*7 Men*	*7 Wenches*	*7 Boys*
Sun	EL (L)	I	S	E
Moon	ME	IH	AB	AN
Venus	ESE	ILR	ATH	AVE
Jupiter	IANA	DMAL	IZED	LIBA
Mars	AKELE	HEEOA	EKIEI	ROCLE
Mercury	AZDOBN	BEIGIA	MADIMI	HAGONEL
Saturn	STIMCVL	STIMCVL	ESEMELI	ILEMESE
Direction of reading in square	NE	SW	NW	SE

The procedure is hardly mystifying, if we ignore for the moment the claimed spiritual transmission. The names are those used in the construction of the wax seals (the Sigillum Emeth and four others) used by Dee in invocations. The procedure for generating these names would have seemed logical and proper to Dee, as qabalist and mathematician — though his mathematical sense must have been upset by the lack of symmetry in the directions for reading the planetary names. (The desire for symmetry would be better satisfied if either the first or second column were read in in the opposite direction — with LVCMITS as the name of a spirit of Saturn).

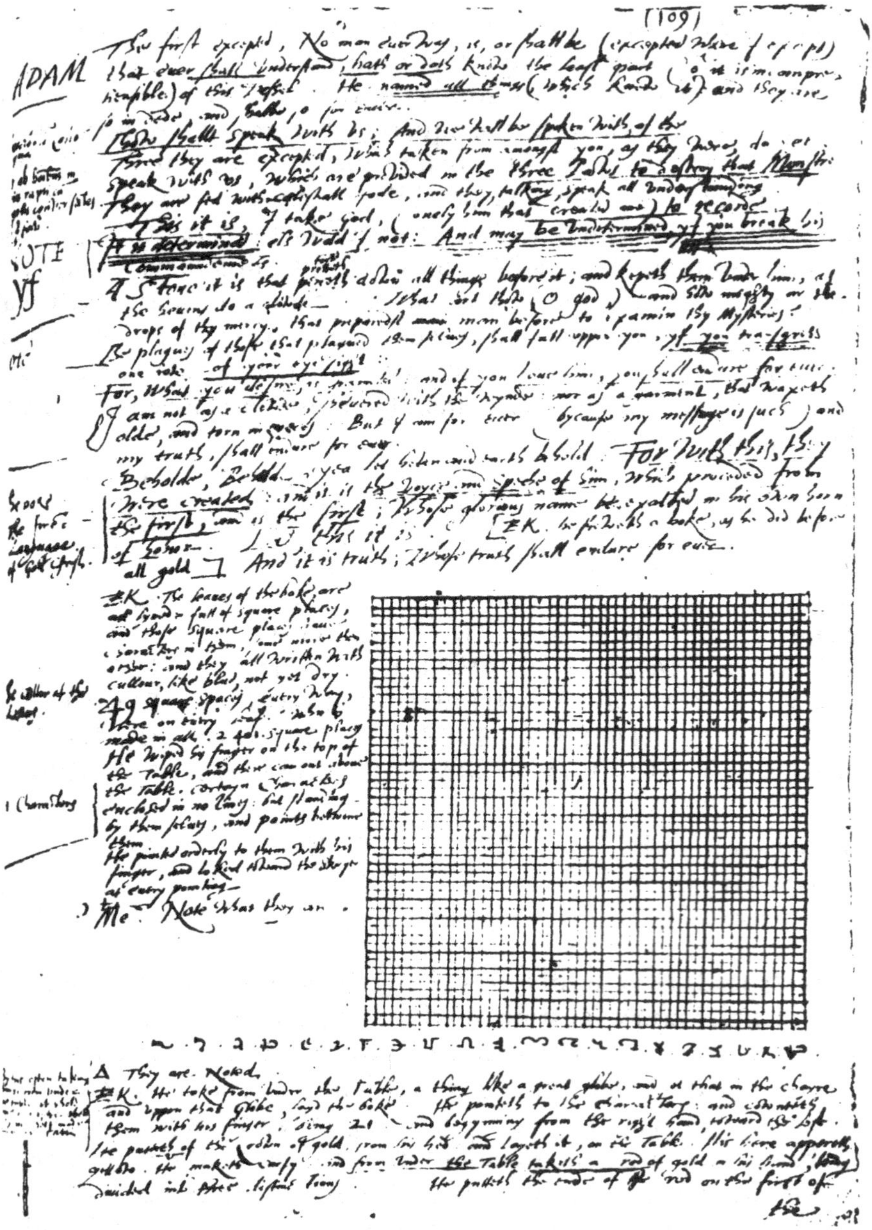

Dee's record of the skrying session for 26 March 1583 when the Enochian letters first appeared, in Sloane MS 3188, f.64. (Courtesy of the British Library).

But what is surprising is that never again, in the seven years of seances that followed, do we get a clear picture of the formation of a square from previously-known elements — and only rarely are we in a position to say with certainty just how names have been generated from the squares. Almost a hundred further squares are dictated by the spirits, some of them as large as 49×49; some are dictated straight across, letter by letter, others are created by the rearrangement of previously-dictated squares. But the details of their creation become increasingly baffling — either because the procedure is increasing in complexity, or because Dee is no longer bothering to set down the details for himself, or both. If the Enochian language is generated by some systematic process from squares, whether as a cipher or as a set of mystical words, we do not have the method.

The appearance of the Enochian alphabet

Just after the dictation of the squares discussed above, on 26 March 1583, Edward Kelley produced the first material concerning the 'angelicall language'. On that day he has a vision of a magical book, with the leaves, perhaps inevitably, 'all filled with squares'. The dictating of the contents of this book occupies the seances of the next thirteen months — with some interruptions, in which the spirits dictate other matter, or prophesy, or refuse to appear at all. There is also some interference from non-angelic spirits, mostly of the type that occultists would recognise as elementals.

First of all, the alphabet of the new language appears: twenty-one special characters, each with its own name. The character names are odd, and seem to bear no relation to the phonetic value of the character; but the fact that the names were given in three groups of seven, and total in all 64 letters, may suggest that here again there may be a square concealed: 8×8, or perhaps even 7×9 or 21×3.

The characters appear three times in the manuscript record of this session: once without the names, once with the names, and once as a fair copy, in a slightly different form. They are also repeated, in their final and most stylised form, at the end of the whole sequence, over a year later; there is also a fair copy by Kelley in the manuscript *Liber Mysteriorum Sextus et Sanctus*

(Sloane MS. 3189), which is a very sloppy transcript of the contents of the angelic book. In addition, individual words written in the characters, in the handwriting of both Kelley and Dee, appear sporadically throughout the manuscripts.

It is necessary to compare all these versions to get a real idea of the characters. The first two versions, for example, look much more like Dee's Hebrew characters than later versions (the letters named Veh (C), Ged (G), Graph (E), and Fam (S) are identical with Aleph, Cheth, Daleth and Resh). The direction of writing, like that of all Semitic languages, is from right to left, but my attempts to trace this alphabet back to a specific Semitic source have failed. All that can be said is that the characters have a general appearance rather like Samaritan — though their stylised forms may also suggest Ethiopic. The scripts they do *not* resemble are proto-Semitic, or Egyptian hieroglyphic, or Sumerian — a resemblance that would seem essential if we were to believe that the script, like the angelical language, dated back to 'before the Flood', and was the most ancient script of mankind.

We may seek a plausible explanation for the 'angelical' script in the fact that Dee may well have had in his library ancient manuscripts in a writing that he could not read, and that either he or Kelley could have got the idea from such a source. Moreover, the idea of the 'lost book of Enoch' (mentioned in the Bible at Jude 14) was very much in the air in the sixteenth century; it is mentioned in several Christian commentaries on the qabalah. The first manuscripts of this work, supposed lost throughout all the Middle Ages, were not found until the middle of the seventeenth century, in Ethiopic and Greek versions. Could Dee perhaps have been in possession of an Ethiopic version of the *Book of Enoch* — which he would certainly not have been able to read?

Another clue to the origin of the Enochian script is given by a sixteenth century work on alchemy: the *Voarchadumia* of Pantheus (1530). On page 12-13 of this work we find another alphabet called Enochian; it is perhaps not additionally surprising, though it seems never to have been pointed out before, that the British Museum copy of this work had actually belonged to Dee, as early as 1559, as attested by the copious marginal notes. Dee's Enochian alphabet bears no relation to that in Pantheus, but Pantheus may have provided the idea. It seems, in the absence of any other evidence, that the Dee/Kelley alphabet may be fanciful, based perhaps on subconscious recollection of similar scripts in earlier literature. There is certainly nothing in Casaubon's suggestion, in his edition of the Dee diaries, that the characters 'are no other, for the most part but such as were set out and published long agoe by one *Theseus Ambrosus* out of Magical books'. The reference is to a work published in 1539 (*Introductio in Chaldaicam linguam,* by Theseus Ambrosius Albonesius), in which are contained a large number of alphabets, both real and magical; and not one of the alphabets resembles Enochian in any way.

The first 'angelical' language

In any case, it is by means of these characters that the first texts in the 'angelical language' are dictated a few days later (29 March 1583 — Good Friday, as it happened to be). In the very first instance, the archangel Raphael *names* the letters, and Dee writes down these names (as if a Greek word, say λογος, were dictated and written down by the Greek letter names *Lambda Omicron Gamma Omicron Sigma*). Afterwards, Dee wrote out the English letters corresponding to the characters, and then read back the text for checking by the angelic visitors.

But after the first two texts, Dee began to realise that the method was much too slow, considering the amount of material yet to come:

> 'Yf euery side conteyne 49 rows, and euery row will require so much tyme to be receyued as this hath done it may seme that very long time will be requisite to this doctrine receyuing. But if it be gods good liking, we wold fayne haue some abridgment or compendious manner, wherby we might the sooner be in the work of Gods seruyce.'

By this remark we see again that the 'texts' really represent further squares. Each text is in fact one line of a gigantic 49×49 square, each square containing one word; there are two sets of such texts, or 98 in all. The physical difficulties of constructing a square so large, and fitting it on to one leaf of a book, daunted even Dee and Kelley.

We can just take each line of the square as being a text, and for

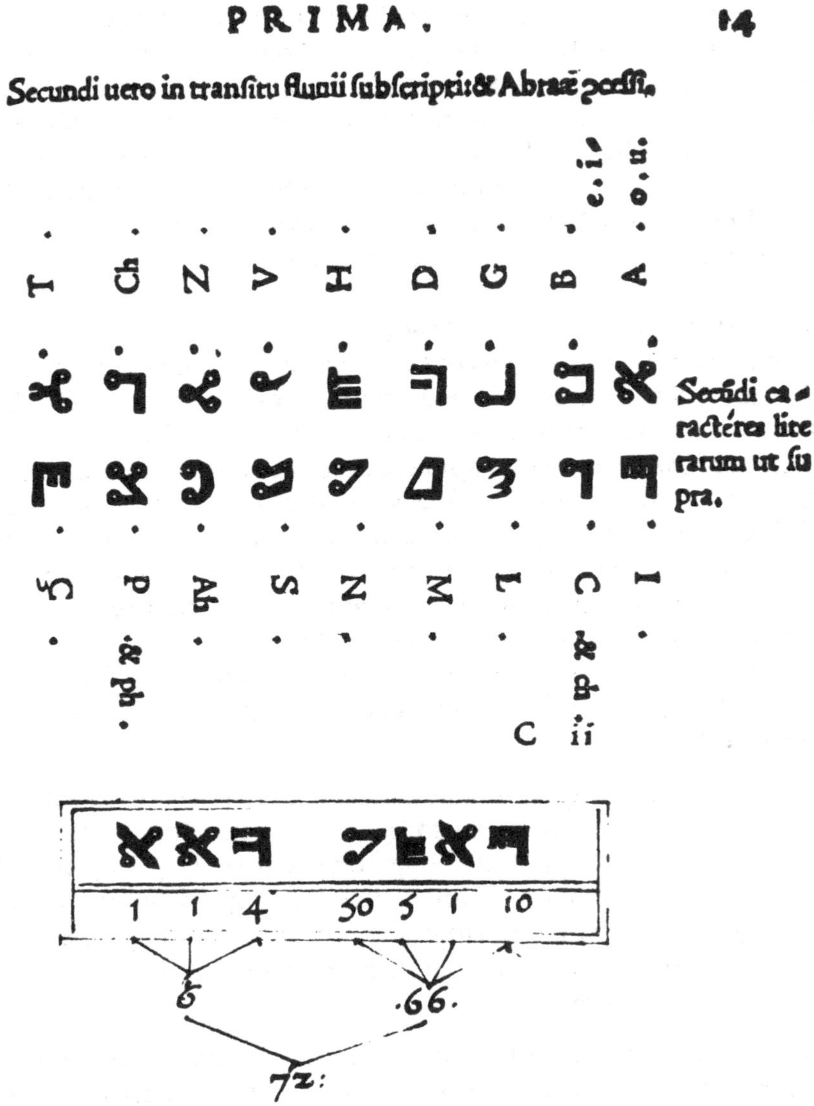
PRIMA. 14

Secundi uero in transitu fluuii subscripti & Abrae possi.

Secũdi caractéres literarum ut supra.

C ii

1 1 4 50 5 1 10

6 .66.

72:

Pages 14-15 from the copy of the *Voarchadumia* by Pantheus given to John Dee on 18 January 1559, showing an 'alphabet of

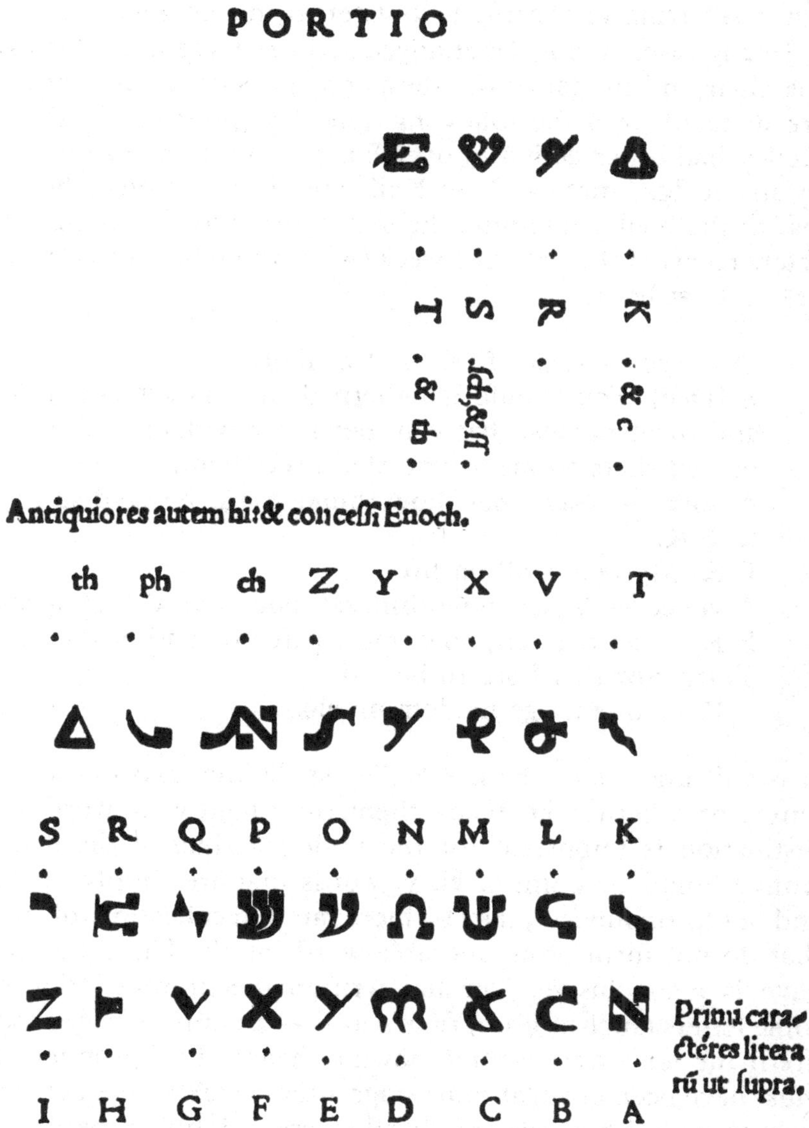

Enoch' and Dee's manuscript note deriving the numerical value of his name written in these characters.

easy identification number them from 1 to 49, with the prefix I or II indicating whether the first or second square is meant, when referring to specific texts later in this chapter.

In any case, the angel is annoyed at the request, and whips away the chair and the table; the shewstone goes dark. No more texts are dictated until the following Tuesday (presumably Dee and Kelley had other activities over Easter), and then, as requested, by an abridged method. Now Kelley receives a vision of the whole leaf of the book containing the text, written in the strange characters received the previous week (with which he is obviously not yet quite at home):

> 'A voyce — Read. E.K. — I cannot.
> Δ [Dee]: You should haue lerned the characters perfectly and theyr names, that you mowght now haue redily named them to me as you shold see them.
> A voyce — Say what thow thinkest. Δ: he sayd so to E.K.
> E.K. My hed is all on fire.
> A voyce — What thow thinkest, euery word that speak.
> E.K. I can read all, now, most pefectly, and in the Third row this I see to be red.
> Palce duxma ge na dem oh elog . . .'

It is still uncertain whether Kelley spells the texts out letter by letter, or whether he reads them off fluently as words. The distinction is important for the understanding of the material from a linguistic point of view; words that are simply 'spelled', and not 'pronounced', may be mere random collections of letters, that do not form pronounceable words at all. The evidence we have is inconclusive. Dee has written the pronunciation over some letters (such as *g* as *j*, final *u* as *f*) — an unnecessary procedure if the texts were written down as heard. This pronunciation must have been given at some stage after the texts were delivered, even though the angels specifically forbid 'dubble repetition', or reading over the text after it is dictated — the quote on page 37 gives the reason.

On the other hand, the pronounceability of the words of the texts speaks in favour for a theory of the words having been read out one after the other, without spelling. There are no sounds that would give any trouble to a native speaker of English, and only a few difficult combinations (*bdrios, excolphabmartbh, longamphlg, lapch*). And some of the texts run so fluently, with so much repetition, rhyme, alliteration, and other types of phonetic patterning, that we are almost forced to conclude that, in the later texts at least, Kelley was speaking aloud, and probably at normal speech speed:

I.13 Ampri apx ard ardo arga arges argah ax...
I.23 ...arcasa arcasam arcusma...
I.24 ...umas ges umas umas ges umas umas ges gabre umas umascala umphazes umphagam masga mosel...
I.25 ...zimah zemah zumacah...zapne zarvex zorquam ...zimagauna zonze zamcha...
I.26 ...zambuges zambe ach oha zambuges gasca lunpel zadphe zomephol zun zadchal...
I.37 ...gasmat gasque gasla gasna gasmaphes gasmagel gasnunabe...

Text II.20 alternates one- and two-syllable words for thirty three words in succession, with one trifling exception; and an even more subtle form of patterning is found in II.24, where there is a strong tendency (broken only by minor exceptions) for monosyllables containing *o* or *u* to alternate with disyllables containing the same vowel (mostly *a*) repeated with a nasal consonant:

II.24 Voh gemse ax pah losquan nof afma ol vamna un samses oh set, quamsa ol danfa dot fanta on anma ol...

What are we to make of this phonetic patterning? Statistical studies in linguistics show that patterning of this nature is rare in normal language — though it is found in poetry and magical charms. It is also characteristically found in certain types of meaningless language (such as glossolalia), which is often produced under conditions similar to trance.

In other words, Kelley may have been 'speaking in tongues'. He did apparently go into trance, as we see from numerous notes in Dee's record of the seances:

> 'Now the fire shot oute of E.K. his eyes, into the stone, agayne. And by and by he vnderstode nothing of all, neyther could reade any thing: nor remember what he had sayde.'
>
> 'The fire cam from E.K. his eyes, and went into the stone agayn. And then; he could not perceyue, or reade one worde.'
>
> 'Suddenly there cam the fyre from his eyes into the stone agayne. And then he could say no more: nor remember any thing of that he had herd, seen or vnderstode less than half a quarter of an howre before.'
>
> [2-3 April 1583]

There are also a few passages which tend to suggest that Kelley did speak the language fluently, instead of reading it letter by letter:

> 'But E.K. prayed perfectly in this Angels language.'
>
> [2 April 1583]
>
> 'A voyce — One Note more, I haue to tell thee.
> Ax him not what he sayeth, but write as thow hearest: for it is true.
> Δ. Then, o lord, make my hearing sharp and strong, to perceyue sufficiently as the case requireth.
> Rap[hael] — Be it vnto the.
> Then E.K. red as followeth' [text I.22 follows]
>
> [3 April 1583]

If we take this as evidence that Kelley was saying 'words' rather than 'letters', then there is no evidence to suggest that these early invocations are any form of 'language' — in the sense of texts bearing a translatable meaning — at all. All the facts seem compatible with Kelley pouring out a string of gibberish while in a trance state. Nevertheless, Dee does add to some of the words some puzzling translations in the margin — but I think he could not have translated a whole text. A few of these glosses are interesting:

> *gassagen* the divine powre creating the angel of the same
>
> *tohcoth* this name comprehendeth the number of all the fayries, who are diuels next to the state and condition of man
>
> *apachana* the slimie things made of dust
>
> *donasdogamatastos* the furious and perpetuall fire enclosed for the punishment of them that are banished from the glory

Whatever else, it is an economical tongue.

So much for the 'language' which makes up *Liber Logaeth,* or the 'Book of the Speech from God', which exists in Kelley's handwriting in the British Museum as Sloane MS. 3189. Kelley's text shows a number of discrepancies from Dee's (as far as it goes), which I take to be evidence of his general carelessness in such matters; but perhaps the conditions he had to work under were not ideal:

> 'As E.K. was writing the *eighteenth leafe, which was of the spirites of the earth,* (in the afternone about 4½ of the clok) he red a parcell thereof, playnely and alowde to him self, and therevpon suddainely at his side appeared three or fowr spirituall creatures like laboring men, having spades in theyr hands, & theyr haires hanging about theyr eares, and hastely asked E.K. what he would haue, & *wherefore he called* them. He answered that he called them not. And they replyed, & said, that he called them; and he replyed & said, that he called them not, and they replyed & said, that he called them: Then I began to say, they lyed: for his intent was not to call them, but onely to read & repeat that which he had written: and that *euery man who readeth a prayer to perceyue the sence*

thereof, prayeth not. No more, did he call them. And I bad them be packing out of the place. And thervppon remoued from my desk (where I was ruling of Paper for his writing) to the grene Chayre, which was by my Chymney; and presently he cryed out & sayd, *they had nipped him, & broken his left arme by the wrist:* and he shewed the bare arme and there appeared both on the vpper side and the lower side imprinted depe in, two Circles and broad as Grotes thus  very red: and I seeing that, sowght for a stik, and in the meane while, *they assalted him,* and he rose and cryed to me (saying) they come flying on me, they come; and he put the stole, which he sat on, betwene him & them. But still they cam gaping, or gyrning at him. Then I axed him where they were: and he poynted to the place, and then I toke the stik and came to the place, and in the name of Jesus commaunded those Baggagis to avoyde, & smitt a cross stroke at them, and presently they avoyded.

All thanks be to the onely one Almighty & everlasting God, whose name be praysed now and foreuer. Amen.'

[15 April 1583]

Nevertheless, Kelley did complete his transcript of the book, the last page being written in 6 May 1583, when Dee was away in London. The last leaf of Kelley's transcript contains the 'correct' form of the Enochian characters, and this is how they were conveyed:

'. . . it is to be Noted, that, when E.K. could not aptly imitate the forme of the Characters, or letters, as they were shewed: that they appered drawn on his paper with a light yelow cullor, which he drew the blak vppon, and so the yellow cullor disapearing there remayned onely the shape of the letter in blak. . .'

[6 May 1583]

The 'yellow cullor', whatever it was, is not apparent on the manuscript page today.

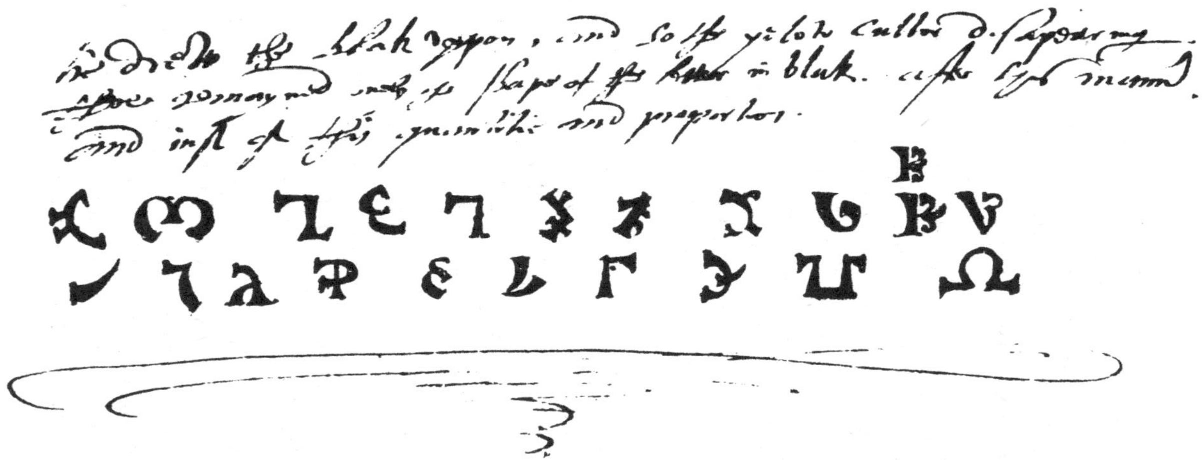

The corrected form of the Enochian letters as they appear in Sloane MS 3188, f.104. (Courtesy of the British Library).

Further seances

Other entries in the *Libri Mysteriorum* at this time deal with quarrels with Kelley (mainly about whether the spirits are good or evil), and the search for treasure and lost cipher-books.

For example, Kelley brought Dee a cipher book supposedly giving the location of buried treasure. Dee works out the cipher — which is quite a simple one — but has trouble in deciding whether one cipher character represents K or X, so he notes in the margin: 'Of this K I dowt yet'. One biographer of Dee (Charlotte Fell-Smith) took this to mean that Dee was distrustful of Kelley! We also find detailed instructions for the magical use of *Liber Logaeth*. All these are matters which need not concern us here. But at the end of the long session of 5 May 1583 Kelley reports a dream which contains accurate predictions of events then four years in the future: the Spanish Armada, and the execution of Mary Queen of Scots. These predictions must be borne in mind when we come to assess the genuineness, or otherwise, of Kelley's mediumship:

> 'Δ. As concerning the Vision which yesternight was presented (vnloked for,) to the sight of E.K. as he sat at supper with me, in my hall, I meane the *appering of the very sea,* and many ships thereon, and the cutting of the *hed of a woman,* by a tall blak man, what are we to imagin thereof?
> Vr[iel] — The one, did signifie the prouision of forrayn powres against the welfare of this land: which they shall shortly put into practise. The other, the death of the Quene of Scotts. It is not long vnto it.'

It may not have been difficult for an intelligent man to guess, at that time, that the execution of Mary Queen of Scots was a likely event, and perhaps a foreign invasion appeared probable even in 1583; but, nevertheless, this stands out as a remarkably detailed prediction. (Mary was beheaded in 1587, and the Spanish Armada was destroyed off the coast of England in the middle of 1588.)

About this time the record published by Meric Casaubon in 1659 commences; the date of the first published seances is 28 May 1583, and it begins abruptly with the appearance of a little girl spirit of seven to nine years old, named Madimi. This is one of the names taken from the second square of letters received by Dee over a year before (see page 26), so he knows at once that her elder sister is Esemeli. (Dee mispronounces this name as Esémeli, and Madimi corrects it to Eseméli.) Madimi, from the earliest session, is regarded as being a spirit representing the planet Mercury, which is appropriate for a teacher of languages and magical sciences; her name, in fact, derives ultimately from the Hebrew word for Mars, מאדים *ma'adim* — whence also 'Madimiel', the name of the intelligence of Mars used in constructing the square.

Other spirits appear from time to time, some of them taken from the earlier tables; but Madimi — who at times reminds one of the 'little girl' contacts of nineteenth-century mediums — makes constant appearances, almost to the very end of the record. (One biographer of Dee, Richard Deacon, says that Madimi grew up and reached 'womanhood' in the seven years that she appeared to Dee; but I find no evidence of this, and the period is only four years (1583-1587). There is a sketch of Madimi in one of his diaries, in which she looks vaguely nubile — but it must be remembered that Dee could see her only in his imagination.)

The appearance of the true Enochian language

The seances continue with magical instructions, philosophising, prophesying, misunderstandings, and contradictions. The text of a new book is dictated, with a new set of 49 invocations (one of which is 'silent'); this is the 'Enochian' language strictly so called, which is the subject of this volume. The differences between this language and the former one are considerable. Firstly, for the Enochian texts, a translation is provided, a fact which right from the beginning makes it look more like a real language. Secondly, the Enochian language appears to be *generated,* in some way, out of the previous tables and squares of *Liber Logaeth* — generated, in fact, out of the earlier 'angelic' language.

Unfortunately, the details of how the Enochian language is derived from the squares is very unclear. Only for the very first call is the system given in detail, and the details are very obscure. We read:

'A. (Two thowsand and fortene, in the sixth Table, is) D
7003 in the thirteenth Table, is I
A in the 21st Table. 11406 downward
I in the last Table, one less than Number:
a word, Iaida.
You shall
understand, what that Word is before the Sonne go down.
Iaida is the last word of the Call.
H 49 ascending T 49 descending A 909 directly:
O, simply.
H 2029. directly. call it Hoath.'

[13 April 1584]

It is clear that the numbers do not, as some writers have claimed, give the 'row and column' of the table, nor can they give the absolute number of letters in the square (counting consecutively from the top left) as there are only 2401 squares (49×49) in each table of *Liber Logaeth,* with each word in the square not exceeding a dozen letters (and the majority much shorter); the numbers in the dictation, however, go as high as 312004.

We can conceive of various ways the letters of the Enochian language can have been taken out of the tables previously given to Dee and Kelley. It is possible, for instance, that the letters of the Enochian texts, joined in order on the squares of *Liber Logaeth,* may form geometrical figures or magical sigils; but there are so many letters to choose from that this approach has proved futile. Other attempts at decipherment, such as that put forward in *The Necronomicon,* London, 1978, researched by Robert Turner and David Langford, and introduced by Colin Wilson, are also unsatisfactory.

The letter-by-letter dictation of the Enochian language does account for some of the differences of this language from the earlier untranslated language. The 'new' language is less pronounceable than the old one, and it has awkward sequences of letters, such as long strings of vowels (*ooaona, mooah*) and difficult consonant clusters (*paombd, smnad, noncf*). This is exactly the type of text produced if one generates a string of letters on some random pattern. (The reader can test this by taking, for example, every tenth letter on this page, and dividing the string of letters into words. The 'text' created will tend to look rather like Enochian.)

But not all Enochian is of this form; many of the words are very pronounceable, as we shall see. The words of the Enochian language itself stop short of having the fully random appearance of the names of God, and of angels and 'kings', that Dee generated from the letters on the squares of his 'elemental tables', that were given later by the spirits — names such as LSRAHMP, LAOAXRP, HTMORDA, ALHCTGA, AAETPIO, which look a lot less plausible, as words of a language, than anything in the Enochian texts.

It is also not completely certain that all the texts in the Enochian language were dictated by the letter-by-letter method. It appears that on at least one occasion Kelley (or the spirits) may have tried to speed up the process, only to be rebuked by Dee's insistence on letter-by-letter transmission. Dee tells Kelley that 'unlesse of this strange language I should have these words delivered unto us letter by letter, we might erre both in Orthography, and also for want of the true pronunciation of the words' (19 April 1584).

The nature of the Enochian language

No matter what the method of transmission was, there are certain observations that we can make about the Enochian language, in the texts that we have. We know something of the pronunciation, from the fact that Dee often wrote the pronunciation of individual words next to the Enochian text. And this Enochian text, written in the Roman alphabet, purports to be a transliteration of the Enochian characters of the text of the original book seen in Kelley's vision. As far as we can tell, each letter of the Roman alphabet transcription represents one Enochian character — which means that Enochian spelling, too, has 'hard' and 'soft' values for *c* and *g*, and combines letters such as *s* and *h* to make the *sh* sound. Very English behaviour for a language 'which Adam verily spake in his innocency, and was never uttered nor disclosed to man since till now' (21 April 1584).

If the phonology of Enochian is thoroughly English, the grammar is no less so. But here we are faced with one difficulty: the nature of the translation. The English rendering of the

Enochian calls is very free, often using five or six words where the Enochian has one; thus, the word for 'man' (or 'reasonable creature') is glossed as 'the reasonable creatures of Earth, or Man'. Proper names, such as *Idoigo* (one of the 'Names of God') are given translations: 'of Him that sitteth on the holy Throne'. Particles, prepositions, and pronouns are filled in where the sense requires them, but we do not know exactly what they are supposed to represent in Enochian; *moooah,* for example, is glossed as 'it repenteth me' — but it could just as easily be an active verb ('I regret').

Moreover, of about 250 different words in the Enochian texts, more than half occur only once, so that we have no real check on their form or meaning. Nevertheless, we can identify a number of different roots, often in quite distinct forms: *om* 'understand, know', *oma* 'understanding', *omax* 'knowest', *ixomaxip* 'let be known'. This is probably the most language-like, and least explicable, feature of Enochian. What is less certain, however, is how much the differences in the spellings reflect the grammar of Enochian; we find, for example, *caosg, caosga* 'earth', *caosgi* 'earth (accusative case)', *caosgin* 'than the earth', *caosgo* 'of earth', *caosgon* 'to the earth' — but are these really case endings, or just chance variants? The same case endings are not found from one noun to another, so that there are either a large number of different declensions (as in Latin or Greek), or else there are no case-endings at all. I incline toward the latter view.

The vocabulary elements of the language are probably arbitrary; certainly they do not seem to be directly derivable from anything in English, Latin, Greek or Hebrew. But in some cases we meet words we half recognise, with unfamiliar meanings: *angelard* 'thought' (from 'angel'?), *babalond* 'wicked, harlot' (from 'Babylon'?), *christeos* 'let there be' (from 'Christ'?), *levithmong* 'beasts of the field' (a blend of 'Leviathan' and 'mongrel'?), *luciftias* 'brightness' (from 'Lucifer'?), *nazarth* 'pillars of gladness' (from 'Nazareth'?), *paracleda* 'wedding' (from 'paraclete'?), *paradial* 'living dwellings', *paradiz* 'virgins' (both from 'Paradise'?), *salman* 'house' (from 'Solomon'?). (Note that most of the suggested origins are proper names, and are biblical — whatever conclusions may be drawn from that.) The remaining words do not seem to have any assignable etymology, though one can be seduced by occasional plausible explanations, such as *micaolz* 'mighty' from Scots *mickle,* or *izizop* 'vessels, containers' from Hebrew אשישות *'ăšišot* 'vessels'.

It is hard to be dogmatic about Enochian grammar. Verbs show singular and plural forms, and present, future, and past tenses, and have also some participial and subjunctive forms; but we do not have a full declension of any verb.
The fullest data is that for the verbs 'say' and 'be', as follows:

gohus	'I say'	*zir, zirdo*	'I am'
gohe, goho	'he says'	*geh*	'thou art'
gohia	'we say'	*i*	'he/she/it is'
gohol	'saying'	*chiis, chis, chiso*	'they are'
gohon	'they have spoken'	*as, zirop*	'was'
gohulim	'it is said'	*zirom*	'were'
		trian	'shall be'
		christeos	'let there be'
		bolp	'be thou!'
		ipam	'is not'
		ipamis	'cannot be'

Not much to build a grammar on. We can in addition identify some of the pronouns (*ol* 'I'; *ils* 'thou'; *tox, tbl* 'of him'; *tia* 'his'; *pi* 'she'; *tibl* 'her (acc.)'; *tiobl* 'in her'; *tilb* 'of her'; *z* 'they'), a few more verb forms, and four ways of expressing negation (*chis ge* 'are not'; *ip uran* 'not see'; *ri-pir* 'no place'; *ag toltorn* 'no creature'). But it is apparent that there is nothing strikingly un-English about the grammar: no trace of the construct case or irregular plurals of Hebrew or Arabic, no clear indication of multiple cases or complex verb forms, as in Latin and Greek. The grammar further suggests English with the removal of the articles ('a' and 'the') and the prepositions — and with a few irregularities thrown in to confuse the picture.

The order of words is also strongly English. A phrase such as *adrpan cors ta dobix* 'cast down such as fall' is pure English in its order, and can not idiomatically be duplicated in four words with these meanings in any other European or Semitic language.

However, this language with an English base was not dictated in English-speaking surroundings, but in Cracow in Poland —

part of Dee's six-year absence abroad, living on foreign patronage. (Kelley never returned to England.) But it would be futile to look for Polish influence in Enochian — especially as all the scholars with whom Dee and Kelley were in contact spoke Latin.

There is one aspect of Enochian 'grammar' that remains totally inexplicable: the number system. Throughout the Calls, various numbers occur, and with a certain amount of extrapolation it seems possible to identify most of the numerals from 'one' to 'nine':

0 — T
1 — L, EL, L-O, ELO, LA, LI, LIL
2 — V, VI-I-V, VI-VI
3 — D, R
4 — S, ES
5 — O
6 — N, NORZ
7 — Q
8 — P
9 — M, EM
10 — X

However, the system that generates the remaining numbers is a complete mystery. A full list of the numbers occurring in the Enochian Calls is given here:

12 — OS
19 — AF
22 — OP
24 — OL
26 — OX
28 — OB, NI
31 — GA
33 — PD
42 — VX
456 — CLA
1000 — MATB
1636 — QUAR
3663 — MIAN
5678 — DAOX
6332 — ERAN
6739 — DARG
7336 — TAXS
7699 — ACAM
8763 — EMOD
9639 — MAPM
9996 — CIAL
69636 — PEOAL

The test of any future spirit-revelation of the Enochian language will be the explanation of this numerical system.

The pronunciation of Enochian

As the texts dictated in Enochian consist of a series of 'Calls', or invocations of supernatural beings, it was clearly necessary for Dee and Kelley to know how the words should be uttered; in most magical systems, a slight error in the text of a spell or invocation is regarded as potentially leading to disastrous consequences. Accordingly, Dee was in the habit of writing the pronunciation of the Enochian words alongside the text. If Kelley dictated the words letter by letter, he must have provided the pronunciation of the whole word immediately afterward.

To make these observations on pronunciation, Dee had to make shift with the ordinary English alphabet; he had no system of phonetic notation. But his intention is usually quite clear. He writes *dg* when he means 'soft *g*' (as in *gem*); and *s* for 'soft *c*'; and he indicates in some places that *ch* is to be pronounced as *k*. He marks the stressed vowels in most words. Sometimes — but not often — he indicates that a letter is to be given its pronunciation in the alphabet — thus *ds* is to be pronounced 'dee ess', and *z* in a few instances is given the pronunciation 'zod'. (The letter *z* has not always been called 'zed' or 'zee'; it has had many names, among them being 'izzard', and, at the end of the sixteenth century, 'ezod'. 'Zod' is nothing but a variant of this last name.) In more difficult cases, he gives examples from English, thus, *zorge* is said to be pronounced to rhyme with 'George', and *ul* to be said 'with such sound to U as we pronounce yew, whereof bows are made' — that is, *ul* is pronounced like 'Yule'.

With all of these instructions we can get a fairly good idea of how Enochian sounded to Dee and Kelley. We have to make allowances, of course, for the fact that the two men spoke English of more than four centuries ago — and also that, while Dee came from the Midlands, Kelley came from Worcestershire, at a time when the dialect variations in England were greater than they are now. Fortunately, linguists are in the possession of sufficient evidence — in the forms of pronunciation guides in schoolbooks, rhymes, misspellings, and the like — to establish the pronunciation of most forms of Elizabethan English with a high degree of accuracy (passages of Shakespeare, for instance, have been published in phonetic transcription, representing Shakespeare's own pronunciation).

The resulting pronunciation of Enochian makes it sound much more like English than it looks at first sight. The following table of letters and combinations gives a general view of how the spelling system of Enochian worked:

Letter	Pronunciation
A	— long (stressed), as in *lah-di-dah*
	— short (unstressed), as in French *patte*
B	— usually as English *b*, but silent between *m* and another consonant, or after *m* finally
C	— as *k* before *a, o, u* (with some exceptions)
	— as *s* before *i, e* (with many exceptions), and in clusters of consonants (*noncf=nonsf*)
CH	— as *k* in most positions, but as *ch* finally
D	— as *d* in all positions
E	— when stressed, as in French *fee*
	— when unstressed, as in *bed*
F	— as *f* in all positions
G	— as (hard) *g* before *a, o, u*
	— as *j* before *i, e,* in final position, after *d,* and in clusters of consonants
H	— as *h* in most positions (except in combinations *ch, ph, sh, th*); silent after a vowel, but the vowel is lengthened
I	— when stressed, as in (French) *machine*
	— when unstressed, as in *bit*
	— in combinations: *ai* as in *fly; ei* as in *eight; oi* as in *boil*
	— as *y* in word-initial position before a vowel (*Iad=Yad*)
K	— as *k* in all positions
L	— as *l* in all positions
M	— as *m* in all positions
N	— as *n* in all positions
O	— when stressed, as in French *mot*
	— when unstressed, as in *not*
	— in combinations: *oi* as in *boil; ou* as in *bout; oo* as in *fool*
P	— as *p* except in combination *ph*

PH	— as *f*
Q, QU	— as *kw* (*qu* in *quick*) — but the word *q* is pronounced *kwa*
R	— as *r* in *right* (but may be rolled)
S	— usually as *s* in *sit*
	— sometimes *z*, in places where this is more natural in English (*lrasd*=*elrazd*)
SH	— as *sh* in *ship*
T	— as *t* except in combination *th*
TH	— as *th* in *thank*
U	— as *oo* in *boot,* or *u* in *put*
	— in initial position as *yew*
	— as *v* or *w* before another vowel, and in word-final position
X	— as *x* in *fox*
Y	— as *y* in word-initial position before a vowel
	— as the letter I before a consonant, and in word-final position
Z	— as *z* in *zoo;* in a very few words, as *zod*

It should be further noted that the Enochian characters themselves total only 21, not the 24 characters listed above; C and K are expressed by a single letter, as are I and Y, and U and V. The 21 letters of Enochian are, oddly enough, almost exactly the minimum required to write English without any ambiguity; perhaps Dee was interested in spelling reform.

Using the punctuation guide above, we can transcribe the beginning of the Call of the Aethyr LIL (as given on page 268) into an approximate phonetic representation:

> Mádriaks di-es praf lil kis miká-olz sánir ka-ózgo od físis balzízras yaida. Nonsa gohúlim: míkma adóyan mad, yá-od bliórb, soba o-áona kis lusíftias pirípsol, di-es abrása nonsf netá-ib ka-ozji, od tilb adfát dámploz...

As we shall see below, Enochian acquired a very different pronunciation when it came to be used in nineteenth-century magical rituals; but for the moment we are concerned with Dee and Kelley.

Dee and Kelley — the last years

Throughout the remaining years of the association of Dee and Kelley we have, in the record of the seances, a fascinating documentation of the character of the two men, which is relevant to any judgment we may wish to form on Enochian. Though the diaries give only the viewpoint of Dee, the characters of both men come through clearly. Dee is credulous, and willing, usually, to give the spirits the benefit of the doubt; but he keeps a close watch on them too, and queries them when he catches them out in a discrepancy. (The spirits chide him time and time again for asking so many questions — awkward questions.) Kelley, on the other hand, is often surly, and largely uninterested in what the spirits are transmitting through him, except where he sees a chance to find out how to work his alchemical powder, and turn base metal into gold. On one occasion, apropos of nothing, he interrupts the girl-spirit Madimi with the question: 'Canst thou, Madimi, lend me a hundred pounds for a fortnight?' — only to be told, roughly enough, that 'I have swept all my money out of doors'.

Kelley apparently wanted the money in order to clear out, and abandon Dee. A few days before this request, on 29 June 1583, the spirits, speaking through Kelley, warned Dee about this intended departure. The warning was in Greek, which Dee understood well enough, but Kelley certainly did not; he says to the spirit Madimi: 'Unlesse you speak some language which I understand, I will expresse no more of this Ghybbrish'. Madimi also announces: 'It is the Syrian tongue you do not understand it'; can Kelley be trying to throw Dee off the scent here? This episode provides evidence of Kelley speaking yet another language he could not know consciously — and here, if we are to believe that he faked the episode, we must still endeavour to explain how or where, in London at that epoch, he could have learned the necessary Greek phrases. (Kelley was even supposed to be ignorant of the Greek alphabet; in his regular diaries, Dee used to write English in Greek letters, whenever he had something to hide from the prying eyes of Kelley. I am not entirely convinced, however, that a sharp man like Kelley would not have penetrated this device.)

Kelley perhaps wished to leave because the first date announced for the performance of the 'Enochian' magic (August 1583) is close at hand, and he does not want to be around in case it is a fiasco; but it is still hard to see why (and how) he would deliver a message against himself in a language he did not know.

Be that as it may, Kelley is persuaded to stay (with a pay rise), and the spirits continue their instruction. They dictate pages of letters and symbols which seem to lead nowhere, and fill up even more pages with vague prophesying that resembles the sermons of a third-rate evangelical preacher. Their practical knowledge tends to be earthly rather than supernatural, and they have read the same books as Dee and Kelley. (For example, the spirits dictate a list of 91 parts of the earth, ruled by 91 'princes', in the Enochian system of magic; Kelley turns up next day and announces, in some agitation, that the complete list can be found in 'a book of Agrippa's'. The question that immediately arises is: did Kelley make this announcement to forestall a discovery that Dee would eventually make?)

The spirits show many of Kelley's limitations, in imagination and thought; and they tend to identify the many books on Dee's shelves by the characteristics of their bindings, and not by their titles or contents. They have also been poking around in the hidden recesses of the house: on one earlier occasion they announce their knowledge of a record of Dee's seances with previous mediums. Dee had stuffed it up the chimney in an attempt to hide it from Kelley.

On at least one occasion, Kelley can be shown to have falsified the spirit doctrine for his own ends. Almost at the end of the *Libri Mysteriorum*, on 18 April 1587, we find recorded that on the previous day (at a time when Dee was not present) Madimi had suggested to Kelley that the two men share their wives in common — the attractive young Jane Dee, and the almost unknown Joanna Kelley. Dee queries this, and the spirits dictate, as confirmation, a string of numbers in what turns out to be a very elementary cipher. The 624 letters of the large square (24×26) of the 'Elemental Tables' dictated some time before are numbered from 1 to 624, each number designating a letter. The letters dictated spell out the following message in Latin:

> 'Cara tibi uxor, carior tibi sapientia, carissimus tibi ego. Electus tremis, ac hesitando peccas: Noli igitur [hesitare] ad genium, et carnem sapere; sed obtempera mihi: ductor

> enim tuus sum, et auctor spiritus omnibus. Hec omnia a me sunt, et licita vobis.'

Which reads:

> 'Dear to you is your wife, dearer to you is wisdom, dearest to you am I. Though chosen, you tremble, and in hesitating you sin. Do not therefore [hesitate] to know the mind and the flesh; but obey me, for I am your leader, and the creator of all spirits. All these things are from me, and are permitted to you.'

(The Latin text is that yielded by the cipher, with a few literal errors silently corrected. There should be another verb — perhaps *hesitare* — after *igitur*, and *spiritus omnibus* should probably read *spirituum omnium;* but Kelley's Latin was always shaky. For example, the Casaubon edition of the Dee-Kelley seances has *auctor spiritus omnium* at the end of the penultimate sentence — which we could translate, somewhat facetiously, as 'I am the ghost-writer of all'.)

The cipher shows a number of minor errors — apart from the major fault that most of the numbers are one out; Dee's marginal note is 'I perceive that commonly one is to be abated of the number'. It would require a great deal of credulity to ascribe such an error to the angels, rather than to Kelley.

The wife-swapping episode took place, in spite of the attempts of some biographers of Dee to suggest that it did not. In the original manuscripts there is a section, heavily erased and barely legible, recording the seance of 23 May 1587 — the morning after the wife-swapping. The spirits ask Kelley: 'Was thy brother's wife [Jane Dee] obedient and humble unto thee?' — and Kelley replies: 'She was'. Dee returns the same answer concerning Joanna Kelley.

Dee's association with Kelley, and apparently also with the Enochian angels, ended shortly after this episode — perhaps the tensions in that household of two British couples in Bohemia were becoming too much to bear, and Kelley set himself up as an alchemist in a separate establishment. Nevertheless, the Dees did not leave for England until March 1589, arriving there in December of that year. Kelley stayed on at the court of Emperor Rud-

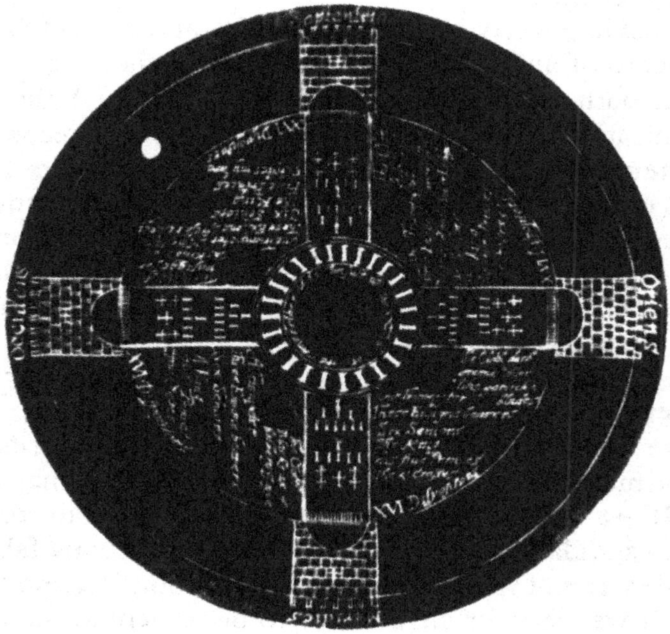

A gold disc engraved with the four Watchtowers shown to Kelley in a dream. (Courtesy of the Trustees of the British Museum).

olph in Prague, and died there in 1595 — under obscure conditions. (The usual story is that he was imprisoned for failing to produce alchemical gold, and fell from a tower when trying to escape.) Kelley was forty at the time — but on 21 August 1584, the angel Uriel had promised that he would live till eighty-seven (and Dee till a hundred and twenty-two). Not even angels are right all the time.

Dee died in poverty in England in 1608, at the age of 81. There is no record of any seance with Kelley after the wife-swapping incident; both men appear to have had enough of the angelic communications. In later life, however, Dee did record a few more attempts of his own; there is a record of a seance in 1607, which is concerned with such mundane matters as his penury and his 'bleeding fundament'. The fantastic angelic revelations seem to have departed with Kelley, and there is no evidence that Dee ever made any use of the Enochian system of magic which he was at such pains to receive.

Judgment on the spirits

What are we to make of all this? Can we accept the spirits at face value, or must we, in a rational age, look for some other explanation? If we insist on a prosaic rationale, there are only two possible candidates for the dubious honour of having fabricated the whole series of spirit-communications: John Dee and Edward Kelley. It was rare for anyone else to be present at the seances, except on a few occasions when Jane Dee and Joanna Kelley turned up to query the wife-swapping incidents.

The spirits, incidentally, show a marked anti-feminist attitude. On 21 March 1585, they rebuke Jane Dee, who has put in a petition for more housekeeping money, 'because she is a woman', and on 23 May 1587 (the morning after the wife-swap) a spirit calling herself 'The Daughter of Comfort' says: 'Disclose not my secrets unto women'.

Dee could certainly have fabricated the whole record. He had the knowledge to do so, and the diaries are in his handwriting; and he delighted in playing with magic squares, circles, and sigils. But such a suggestion must founder on the question: why on earth would he have done so? Only a man clinically insane — and Dee was certainly not that — would have filled many hundreds of pages, covering more than two decades in all, with a private fantasy that became revealed to the world only by accident. The records of the seances were never intended for publication; Dee had enough experience in his life of the dangers of appearing to be a magician, without adding fuel to the fire by making public his actions with spirits. (Already in 1583 a mob, disturbed by his reputation for trafficking with spirits, had raided his house in Mortlake, and destroyed a large part of his library.) Moreover, no-one can read the spiritual diaries, which on internal evidence were written down at the seances themselves, or very soon after, and doubt the sincerity of Dee himself believing in the reality of the spirits.

I think, therefore, that we can acquit Dee of any deliberate fraud or mystification in this matter. It is not so easy to acquit Kelley. All we know of him (and that is not in fact a very great deal) suggests that he was an occult charlatan, an opportunist looking for ways to make a 'quick quid'; and we have seen him on a number of occasions inject his own personality into the spirit communications. He had motive enough; not only the £50 a year he was paid by Dee as a retainer, but also, perhaps, pride in being able to create a magical system that would be accepted by a credulous old man, the opportunity to use Dee's library and alchemical laboratories, the chance to bask in Dee's reflected glory, the perks of free travel on the continent, and the freedom to make a pass at Jane Dee. And even in this last motive there may be more than meets the eye: there could well have been a homosexual component in Kelley's attachment to Dee. Kelley married late, and only when the spirits advised him to, admitting that he himself 'had no natural inclination thereto'; and it is a well-established psychological fact that the attraction of a man for a member of his own sex may manifest itself in a desire to possess the beloved's wife, if the beloved himself is not accessible.

But did Kelley have the knowledge to create all his spirit revelations? The Enochian system shows a much deeper knowledge of the qabalah than Kelley would seem to have possessed — but not necessarily more than he might have been able to glean by a surreptitious reading of Dee's books. Nevertheless, there is a remarkable consistency about the whole system, which for Kelley to have invented would argue a phenomenal memory, or the keeping of notes (which would have been hard to conceal from Dee). The Enochian Calls, for example, are translated in their entirety often days after the original dictation: could Kelley have carried all this in his head, or on pieces of paper small enough to escape Dee's attention? (During the sessions of 14 May 1584, and on some other occasions, the spirit communications become very garbled — is this an indication of Kelley getting his notes out of order?)

Kelley's predictions of future events, and the production of the warning in Greek, also need to be accounted for, in any explanation. In favour of the Kelley-fraud hypothesis, however, is the fact that the communications of the spirits, though consistent, do change over time; and the 'system' tends to fall into watertight compartments. There is little real relationship, for instance, between the earlier *Heptarchia* system of the 49 Good Angels, and the later *Claves Angelicae* system of the Enochian tables. The latter is more thorough-going, and, as we have seen, the associated language is more convincing: can Kelley have got better at producing what was required of him, as time went on? He must have learnt a great deal from living in close contact with Dee, and Dee's credulity would blind him to slight internal contradictions. (Dee does, as we have seen, query inconsistencies as he finds them; but there could have been others that he did not record, perhaps subconsciously repressing them. We have after all only *Dee's* record of the seances.)

Perhaps Kelley was just feeding Dee's own fantasies back to him. Or perhaps again he may have been picking up Dee's subconscious thoughts, by some kind of ESP, and elaborating on them. Or perhaps, after all, the spirits were all they said they were, and the Enochian system of magic is the most powerful of which we have a record in the English language. The reader is invited to make his own judgment; mine appears in the conclusion to this chapter.

Is Enochian a cipher?

One further possibility remains to be considered: that the Enochian texts are really a cipher, and that some other message is concealed in them. The suggestion was first made by Robert Hooke in a lecture to the Royal Society towards the end of the seventeenth century, and has been resurrected by Richard Deacon, a modern biographer of Dee (*John Dee: Scientist, Geographer, Astrologer and Secret Agent to Elizabeth I,* London, 1968). The possibility cannot be immediately discounted; Dee was familiar with ciphers, and had the mathematical sophistication to develop systems to a high degree of complexity. We have noted already two clear-cut instances of cipher in the spiritual diaries: the decipherment of Kelley's treasure-manuscript, and the cipher of the wife-swapping incident. There is another cipher in the diaries that should be mentioned, as an instance of the tortured nature of some of the spirit communication, and as evidence of the types of ciphers then employed.

The communication was received by the magicians in the first part of 1585. A figure of an old man appears and reads in a book of 'Ivory bone' a text interspersed with odd words and garbled syntax:

> 'Take of your Dlasod dignified, and *Luminus,* or from due degrees. Gather or take fiery degree... Notwithstanding, work it diverse dayes multiplying four digestions... And double then Dlasod, and thy... *Rlodnr*... For, until thou watch so continuing it, a holy hour descendeth... Of every work there ascendeth one Audcal, and so every Law *Rlodnr*... And purpose Dlasod, take a *swift* Image, and have the proportion of a most glorious mixture *Audcal* and also *Lulo.* Continue and by office seek *Rlodnr* backward by the red digestion. But he by the common or red *Darr* doth gather most ripest work, purge the last fortene well fixed. Then the four through your [*Rlodnr*]...*Roxtan* finished more together at the lower body by one degree... by *you* for him hold it, for him in one of them...until of the last thing...In him become his red and highest degree of his resurrection through coition... After a while I come again... There is the whole work.'
>
> [17 January 1585]

This is, of course, gobbledygook; but the next day a string of figures is dictated, which are to be set over the words, and then the words arranged in their appropriate numerical order. In spite of many errors in the transmission, Dee finally works it out, and the entry for 20 March 1585 prints the corrected plaintext:

> 'Take common Audcal; purge and work it by Rlodnr of four divers digestions, continuing the last digestion for fourteen dayes, in one and a swift proportion, untill it be Dlasod fixed, a most red and luminous body, the Image of Resurrection.
>
> Take also Lulo of red Roxtan, and work him through the four fiery degrees, until thou have his Audcal: and there gather him.
>
> Then double every degree of your Rlodnr, and by the law of Coition and mixture work and continue them diligently together. Notwithstanding backward, through every degree, multiplying the lower and last Rlodnr his due office finished by one degree more than the highest.
>
> So doth it become Darr, the thing you seek for: a holy, most glorious, red, and dignified Dlasod.
>
> But watch well, and gather him, so, at the highest: For in one hour, he descendeth, or ascendeth from the purpose.
>
> Take hold.'

This is still obscure, but it is now recognisable as an alchemical text, for preparing alchemical gold. Levanael appears and explains that *Audcal* is 'gold', *Dlasod* is 'sulphur', *Roxtan* is 'pure and simple Wine in her self', *Lulo* is 'Tartar, simply of red wine' or mother of vinegar, *Darr* is the philosopher's stone, and *Rlodnr* must be something like 'furnace' — but there is no key to the formation of these strange words.

Perhaps it was the practical application of this strange formula that gave Kelley his reputation as an alchemist able to transmute base metal into gold, a reputation that got him the position of alchemist at the court of the Emperor Rudolph. But in any case we can see that the angelic spirits were not averse to using cipher when the need arose.

Nor, of course, was Dee, even if he were not acting as a 'secret agent' of Queen Elizabeth abroad. Many years before, he had acquired a manuscript copy of Trithemius' *Steganographia*, forty years before it was first printed; and this work not only deals with various cipher systems, but also contains a 'mystical language' (in reality a fairly simple cipher) that in some ways resembles Enochian. What Dee thought of this book is contained in a letter to Sir William Cecil from Antwerp, dated 16 February 1563:

> 'Allready I have purchased one boke, for which a thousand Crownes have ben by others offred, and yet could not be obtained. A boke, for which many a lerned man hath long sowght, and dayly yet doth seeke: Whose use is greather than the fame thereof is spread... A boke for your honor, or a Prince, so meet, so nedefull and comodious, as in humayne knowledge, none could be meeter, or more behofefull.'

But the various keys of Trithemius do not work on either of the mystical languages produced by Kelley. The whole Enochian system, with its complexity of squares filled with letters, would seem to lend itself to both transposition and substitution ciphers of all kinds; yet checks of some of the more likely possibilities have yielded nothing worth following up. There may be a cipher in the first set of untranslated invocations that Kelley produced initially (but then these invocations would not look so much like glossolalia), but I do not believe there can possibly be cipher in the Enochian Calls. Let us see why not.

The Enochian Calls, as we have seen, are accompanied by a translation. If this translation is genuine, then the Calls must represent the enciphered version of this translation, in English or some other plausible language. And, since the words of the Enochian text occur consistently with the same translation, the only kind of cipher possible is substitution (whether simple or polyalphabetic). Transposition ciphers, and ciphers with polyalphabetic substitution, just would not yield the same 'word' consistently.

But simple substitution cannot have been used in the Calls, or they would have been cryptanalysed by now. Simple substitution in any of the likely languages (let us say for argument Latin, Hebrew, Greek, English, or any common European tongue) is completely transparent — and how much more so when the translation is available! Take the word ROR, for example, meaning 'sun', if this were a word in a simple substitution cipher, it must represent a three-letter word in which the first and the last letters are the same. The best candidate is Hebrew שמש meaning 'sun'; but substituting the value of these letters in other words (*e.g.* R in GRAA 'moon') does not yield any further Hebrew words. We could perhaps assume a form of multiple substitution, and try English *sun* or Latin *sol* for ROR, and English *moon* or Latin *luna* for GRAA. The reader is welcome to try this; he will find it leads nowhere. Perhaps even more conclusive, however, is that the letter-frequencies per thousand of the Enochian Calls (as calculated by computer) do not produce a graph resembling that of the letter-frequencies for any of the languages under consideration.

But the most damning case against cipher is the fact that there is a translation at all. What would be the point of writing a text in an elaborate cipher, and then writing the plaintext underneath? It is barely possible, of course, that the translation is a mere blind, and that the Calls contain a totally different enciphered text. But there is a difficulty in this too; it would be extremely difficult (though not entirely impossible) to construct a workable cipher that would first encipher one text, and still yield a consistent 'pseudo-translation' as another text. But Enochian is far too much like the language its translation represents for this to be very likely.

Further, if the magical languages and the squares do contain a cipher, why bother to surround it with all the other material from the spirits: prophecies, dictation, general talk, and indication of breaks for dinner? If Dee had wanted to write messages in cipher, for his own use, he could have done so without creating this elaborate fiction.

I think, therefore, it is possible to assert, with a high degree of confidence, that there is no cipher contained in the 'angelical' language, or in the Enochian Calls.

The later history of Enochian

The use of Enochian as a language after the death of Dee and Kelley, and of the related system of magic, cannot yet be fully documented. But as interest in Dee continues to our own day, it is relevant to sketch in some of the main developments.

Dee died in 1608, in the odour of sanctity, and was buried in the chancel of the church at Mortlake, near his house. Kelley, as we have seen, was already dead. If any of Dee's acquaintances or family — perhaps his son, Arthur Dee, who had once tried to serve as a medium for his father, and later became an alchemist in his own right — continued with the practice of Enochian magic, it was without the seance records, which in the second half of the seventeenth century turned up, rather surprisingly, in a secret drawer of a cedarwood chest that had belonged to Dee.

The papers were discovered in the chest in about 1662 by the wife of a certain Mr Wale. He subsequently gave them to Elias Ashmole in exchange for a copy of the latter's book on the Order of the Garter.

Elias Ashmole (1617-1692) was apparently fascinated by their contents, spending a great deal of effort on reconstructing the Enochian system of magic from the often difficult text. He was probably the first man after Dee to attempt to make contact with Dee's angelic spirits, in a series of seances extending from 1671 to 1676.

As the founder of English freemasonry, Ashmole may have had an even greater significance, in introducing the Enochian system into esoteric freemasonry, and into the English occult tradition in general. However, we do not know for certain whether he did or not, for it is to be some two hundred years before Enochian is mentioned publicly again. It seems that some of the nineteenth-century freemasons with occult interests (such as Frederick Hockley and Kenneth Mackenzie) may have been aware of the Dee manuscripts (by then in the British Museum), but it is unlikely that Enochian magic played any part in masonic rituals.

It was to be another Mason and antiquarian who brought Enochian back into English occultism: Wynn Westcott (1848-1925), one of the founders (in 1888) of the highly influential occult Order of the Golden Dawn. It was certainly Westcott who introduced into the Order the complex system of 'Rosicrucian chess', a divination system blending the Enochian system with Egyptian god-forms and Indian four-handed chess (Chaturanga), on which last Westcott was an expert.

The Enochian Calls, and the general system of Enochian magic, were required subjects of study for the Golden Dawn grade of Adeptus Minor — though it seems that few members of the Order ever knew much about them. Most of the original material (first made publicly available in detail by Israel Regardie in his book on the rituals of the Golden Dawn in 1937-40) is by Westcott, but some notes were also included by Westcott's co-founder of the Order, S. L. MacGregor Mathers. An interesting development is the description of a special pronunciation for Enochian. The advice of 'Sapere Aude' (Wynn Westcott) is as follows:

> 'In pronouncing the Names, take each letter separately. M is prounced Em; N is pronounced En (also Nu, since in Hebrew the vowel following the equivalent letter Nun is 'u'); A is Ah; P is Peh; S is Ess; D is Deh.
>
> 'NRFM is pronounced En-Ra-Ef-Em or En-Ar-Ef-Em. ZIZA is pronounced Zod-ee-zod-ah. ADRE is Ah-deh-reh or Ah-deh-er-reh. TAAASD is Teh-ah-ah-ah-ess-deh. AIAOAI is Ah-ee-ah-oh-ah-ee. BDOPA is Beh-deh-oh-peh-ah. BANAA is Beh-ah-en-ah-ah. BITOM is Beh-ee-to-em or Beh-ee-teh-oo-em. NANTA is En-ah-en-tah. HCOMA is Heh-co-em-ah. EXARP is Eh-ex-ar-peh.'

The note by 'S Rioghail Mo Dhream (MacGregor Mathers) describes essentially the same system, but with some idiosyncratic viewpoints:

> 'Briefly, regarding the pronunciation of the Angelical Language, thou shalt pronounce the consonants with the vowel following in the nomenclature of the same letter in the Hebrew Alphabet. For example, in Beth, the vowel following 'B' is 'e' pronounced AY. Therefore, if 'B' in an Angelical Name precede another as in 'Sobha', thou mayest pronounce it 'Sobeh-hah'. 'G' may be either Gimel or Jimel (as the Arabs do call it) following whether it be hard or soft. This is the ancient Egyptian use, whereof the Hebrew is but a copy, and that many times a faulty copy, save in the Divine and Mystical Names, and some other things.
>
> 'Also 'Y' and 'I' are similar, also 'V' and 'U', depending whether the use intended be vowel or

> consonant. 'X' is the ancient Egyptian power of Samekh; but there be some ordinary Hebrew Names wherein 'X' is made Tzaddi.'

The Egyptology is that of the nineteenth century, and we may suspect that this pronouncing system is of the same period; certainly it is not, as we have seen, the pronunciation used by Dee and Kelley. But it is a practical system for coping with some of the consonant-clusters of the Enochian language, especially the divine Names. In use, the system was modified somewhat; thus, *saanir* 'parts' was apparently pronounced as 'saanire', and not — as the instructions above would suggest — 'Ess-ah-ah-en-ee-reh' or something similar.

The occultist Aleister Crowley took the Enochian system very seriously, and published the text of the Calls, together with the details of making the Enochian magical tablets, in his publication *The Equinox* (1909-1913). His version of the Calls is given in his interpretation of the the expanded Golden Dawn pronunciation; the Call of the Aethyr LIL opens:

> 'Madariatza das perifa LIL cahisa micaolazoda saanire caosago od fifisa balzodizodarasa Iaida. Nonuça gohulime: Micama adoianu MADA faoda beliorebe, soba ooaona cahisa luciftias peripesol, das aberaasasa nonuçafe netaaibe caosaji od tilabe adapehaheta damepelezoda. . .'

(Compare this with the reconstructed 'original' pronunciation given above, page 49.)

Crowley's own experiences with the Angels of the Aethyrs were also published in the *Equinox,* and also later as a separate book, *The Vision and the Voice;* but it is not generally known that he also composed a set of additional conjurations in the Enochian language. These are published in his edition of MacGregor Mathers' translation of the *Goetia* or *Lesser Key of Solomon* — but are omitted from many current editions. This additional Enochian material of Crowley's, be it spirit revelation, inspired re-creation, or linguistic dilettantism, tends to use the words of Enochian found in the Calls, but with some extended meanings and a few apparently original words. A specimen, from the invocation entitled 'Ye constraynte':

'Od commemahé do pereje salabarotza kynutzire
'And I bind thee in the fire of sulphur mingled
fabaonu, od zodumebi pereji od salabarotza:
with poison and the seas of fire and sulphur:
niisa, eca, dorebesa na-e-el od zodameranu
come forth, therefore, obey my power and appear
asapeta vaunesa komesalohé.'
before this circle.'

Since the time of the Golden Dawn and the various later Orders in one way or another related to it — for details of which see Francis King's book on *Ritual Magic in England* — various occult groups have attempted to use the Enochian system to try to establish contact with the spirits seen by Kelley. Some have claimed success, in the form of new Enochian material (both language and magical formulas) that is not for profane ears. It is difficult to judge such claims until they appear in print — but one simple test that can be applied is to ask the adepts if they know the Enochian word for 'seven'.

One group that is known to be using the Enochian Calls is the Church of Satan, headed by Anton La Vey in California. La Vey's *Satanic Bible* prints the Enochian Calls, in a form that makes it quite clear that they are taken from Aleister Crowley's version — but he substitutes the name 'Saitan' wherever the original has 'Iaida' ('The Highest'), and makes other minor modifications in the translation: 'Lord of the Earth' for 'God of Justice', and 'King of Hell' for 'The Highest'. Whether Dee's spirits still respond, I do not know.

Dee's spirits have recently been associated with those from another source, the essentially Sumerian and Akkadian demons of the *Necronomicon,* a fictitious work invented by the American fantasy writer H.P. Lovecraft. In all there have been in excess of half a dozen 'editions' of this title, all of different content: of which the *Necronomicon,* Barnes Graphics, New York, 1977 has drawn on Sumerian and Akkadian sources. In the edition of the *Necronomicon* published by Neville Spearman, London, 1978, there is a purported translation of Dee's *Liber Logaeth.* Readers who have followed this introduction so far will be able to assess the validity of the supposed translation for themselves — but it is a long way from ancient Sumeria to Dee's London, and there is not much evidence that H.P. Lovecraft had more than a fiction writer's knowledge of either.

Occult groups which have been known to use the Enochian system in recent years include, in London, the Order of the Pyramid and the Sphinx, and the Aurum Solis; in the Midlands, the Order of the Cubic Stone; and elsewhere the Luculentus Astrum. It is hoped that the material in the present book may be of assistance to them, and to all such groups who are pursuing researches in this area.

Conclusion

In the preceding pages, the arguments for and against regarding Enochian as a genuine language, and for and against accepting the reality of the angelic spirits supposedly contacted by Dee and Kelley, have been put at some length. I do not think anyone can afford to be dogmatic in this area. As a scholar, I am by temperament inclined to doubt wherever doubt is possible; but I have known well people who have pursued the study of Enochian from the point of view of practical occultism, and who claim that, whatever the origin of the system, it works as practical magic. And I have no particular reason to disbelieve them.

I believe, myself, that a combination of factors produced Dee's angelic communications. I am sure that Kelley went into genuine trance states, in which he saw visions which he faithfully reported; but I am equally sure that at least on some occasions he consciously elaborated on those visions, and at times even invented them, and fabricated messages from the spirits, for his own ends; and that he used, consciously and unconsciously, any information that he picked up from Dee, and relayed it back to him.

Nevertheless, there may be genuine revelations at the core of his reported visions. But I think that real angels would speak a more euphonious and more consistent tongue than Enochian, that they would not make mistakes, and that they would have more of import to transmit to man than the interminable outpouring of 'Enoch his boke'. Shakespeare's Macbeth claimed of his witches that 'they have more in them than mortal knowledge'; it would be hard to make the same claim for Dee's angels. Their limitations are those of Kelley; their occasional sublimities, those of Dee. If the true voice of God comes through the shewstone at all, it is certainly as through a glass darkly.

The element of doubt remains, however, and therefore it is not surprising that in the 27th Invocation to the Good Angels, we find, in the words of the first angelical language, the sequence:

> '. . . lafet vncas laphet vanascor torx glust hahaha . . .'

The spirits may well have the last laugh.

Donald C. Laycock
Canberra, December 1978

SCOPE AND PLAN OF THE DICTIONARY

This dictionary is intended to allow the reader to find the basic meaning of any Enochian word used by Dee (both in his original manuscripts and in the printed version of Casaubon) to which at least a tentative meaning can be assigned. In addition, a few words which are clearly Enochian, but to which no meaning can be assigned at present, are included with the gloss 'meaning unknown'.

The Dictionary also includes Enochian words, principally (but not entirely) from versions of the Enochian Calls, from the following sources (for which see Bibliography):

GD	The Golden Dawn: text of the Calls, with additional variants as used in the rituals, and some angelic and holy names.
AC:C	Aleister Crowley's version of the Calls, with additional magical data, as published in *The Equinox,* Vol.I, Nos.7 & 8.
AC:VV	Enochian words (some of them not from Dee) as used by Aleister Crowley in his invocations of the Aethyrs in *The Vision and the Voice.* (Note: in this book Crowley uses other magical languages which have no connection with Enochian. These have not been included.)
AC:G	Variants of Enochian words in the goetic invocations published by Aleister Crowley as a supplement to MacGregor Mathers' translation of the *Goetia.* (Note: only rarely are these words not identifiable with the words of Dee's Enochian; but there are many misprints and mistranslations.)

Another source of Enochian vocabulary, La Vey's *Satanic Bible,* was examined, but the Enochian here follows AC: C exactly, with only two additional misprints (*mamao* for *momao,* and *gianai* for *ginai*) which were thought too insignificant to include in the Dictionary. However, this publication is remarkable for the liberties it takes with the English text of the Calls, as well as omitting, for some odd reason, all the numerals of the original text.

Words which do not have a source given them in the Dictionary are all from Dee; occasionally a form is identified as C (Casaubon) when it does not tally with the manuscripts. The words from the Calls, which are of course the most important source of Enochian, are provided with an indication of pronunciation, as far as can be determined from Dee's notes, and from the principles outlined in the chapter on Enochian. There remain many uncertainties, however, and some readers may prefer to use the pronunciation as suggested by the spellings of Aleister Crowley or the Golden Dawn rituals, as this now has a relatively long occult tradition.

In giving the pronunciation, the rule has been followed of 'consonants as in English, vowels as in Italian' — this means *u* as in *put,* not (Southern British English) *but.* Long vowels are marked with a bar over them (a, i), and the English murmured vowel (as in the last syllable of *father*) has been represented by ë when no other symbol would do; but it would also be possible to pronounce all sequences of *er, ir* and *ur* as *ër* wherever they occur. Note that the *r,* in Dee's time, would have been pronounced everywhere it occurred; a light Scottish burr sounds good, but an American *r* will suffice.

A note must be added on *zod,* which is frequent in the Aleister Crowley versions of Enochian words. This was simply a short-lived Elizabethan word for the letter *Z* (which we now call *zed* or *zee*). As the letter was used less frequently in Elizabethan English than now, but had a high frequency in Enochian, Dee would often write *zod* over the letter *z,* to remind himself that it was not to be spelt *s.* I think that only rarely did he intend this to suggest a pronunciation with *zod.*

Another characteristic of Elizabethan usage was the (to us) inconsistent writing of *u* and *v,* and to a lesser extent *i* and *j.* Dee almost invariably writes *v* at the beginning of words, and *u* in the middle, whether *u* or *v* (of modern English) was intended. With regard to *i* and *j*, he almost always writes only *i*; *j* appears only as capital *I* or *J*, and at the end of words (mostly Latin). These Elizabethan habits in the spelling of Enochian have given rise to some odd-looking words, such as *vnchi* (where we would now write *unchi*). These anomalies have been regularised in the Dictionary, according to modern spelling conventions.

Also, in accordance with the values of the Enochian alphabet given by Dee, *U* and *V* are placed together in the Dictionary, as are *I* and *Y*. However, *J* is placed with *G* rather than with *I*, since the only Enochian words that have ever been spelled with *J* are the Aleister Crowley versions of words beginning with 'soft g'. Similarly, *K* is included with *C*.

Enochian variants that differ *only* in these spelling alternations (such as *u* for *v*) are not always included separately. Nor are variants that differ only in the use of capitals, hyphens, or spaces. Thus, the reader who has encountered, in Aleister Crowley's *Goetia*, the word *dari-lapa*, will only find listed *darilapa* (which also occurs in the *Goetia*). It is not expected that this will cause the reader any inconvenience in finding words.

All variants are cross-referenced to the best possible form of the word as used by Dee, as far as this can be determined; but where there are many Dee variants, these are usually to be taken as all equivalent.

A few variant words are to be found a line or two away from their true alphabetical place, to avoid multiplying cross-references; thus *butamonu* occurs within the entry *butmon*, and not before it. This should not cause inconvenience; if a word is not found at its strict alphabetical place, simply look a line or two higher or lower.

Variants that appear to arise from miscopying or printers' errors are marked with a following asterisk: thus *coasg** (for *caosg*). Such errors are frequent in all previously published works containing any Enochian material; it is to be hoped that the printer treats this work better.

A fairly comprehensive list of divine and angelic names, mainly from Dee's magical manuscripts, is included, but the reader is warned against regarding this list as complete, in the sense of giving the key to the complete Dee magical system. Only those names actually used by Dee (and, preferably, those used with some frequency) are included. The texts contain instructions for generating many additional names, from the various Enochian tables, but no names have been *generated* for this Dictionary. Also, a large number of angelic names that are given in the Golden Dawn rituals are omitted, as these appear to have been created from the tables in ways not intended by Dee. In addition, only the barest outline of the nature and functions of the various spirits can be given in the Dictionary. The publisher of this volume will be bringing out a complete guide to Enochian magic at a later date.

The Enochian Letter at the beginning of each part of the Angelic-English section of the Dictionary is reproduced in facsimile from the original letters in Dee's manuscript diary for 6 May 1583 (Sloane MS 3188 f.104). For details of how they were formed see the previous chapter, page 38.

PART I
ANGELIC-ENGLISH

A Un

Angelic	Source and Pronunciation	English
a	a	1) in, on, of, with. Cf. *c*, *q*. 2) the.
Aaan		angel, companion of *Anaa*. Also *Aavan*.
Aabco		Divine Name of Five Letters, ruling Air of Water.
Aalco	AC:C	
Aadt		angel, companion of *Taad*.
Aaetpio		Senior of Fire, associated with Mars. Also *Aetpio*.
Aaetpoi	GD	
aaf	ā-f	among, amongst. Cf. *eai*, *oai*.
aai	ā-i	
aao	ā-o	
aaiom	GD, AC:C	= *aai om* 'amongst us'.
aaiome	AC:C	
aala	ā-la	put, place
Aalco	AC:C	= *Aabco*, Divine Name.
Aana		angel, companion of *Anaa*. Also *Aavna*.
Aanaa		angel ruling *Anaa* and companions.
aao		= *aaf*, among.
Aaodt		angel, also known as *Aadt*.
Aaoxaif		Senior of Air, associated with Jupiter.
Aapdoce		Senior of Fire, associated with Venus. Also *Apdoce*.

Aavan		angel, also known as *Aaan.*
Aavna		angel, also known as *Aana.*
Aax		cacodemon, counterpart of the angel *Axir.*
Ab		angel (Filia Filiarum Lucis) associated with Luna.
abai	a-bai	stooping.
Abaiond		Governor of the Second Division of the Aethyr *Pop.*
abaivoninu*	GD	= *abai vovin,* stooping dragon.
Abamo		angel, also known as *Abmo.*
Abaoz		angel, also known as *Aboz.*
abaramig		= *abramg, prepare.*
abaramiji	AC:G	
aberaasasa	AC:C	= *abraasa,* provide.
aberameji	AC:C	= *abramg,* prepare.
aberamiji	AC:G	
Abioro		= *Habioro,* Senior of Air.
Abmo		angel powerful in transformation, ruled by *Aiaoai Oiiit.* Also *Abamo.* Companions are *Bmoa, Moab, Oabm.*
aboapri	a-bo-a-pri	serve. Cf. *booapis.*
aboaperi	AC:C	
Aboz		angel, companion of *Boza.*
abraasa	a-brā-sa	provide, provided.
abraassa	GD, AC:VV	
aberaasasa	AC:C	
abra	AC:VV	

abramg	a-bramg	prepare.
abramig	a-bra-mig	
abaramiji	AC:G	
aberameji	AC:C	
aberamiji	AC:G	
berameji	AC:C	
beramiji	AC:C	
ACAM		7699.
acame	AC:C	
Acar		angel ruled by *Rzionr Nrzfm*. Also *Acrar*. Companions are *Cara, Arac, Raca*.
acaro*	AC:C	see *acroodzi*, beginning.
Acca		angel ruled by *Aourrz Aloai*. Also *Acuca*.
Acmbicu		Senior of Earth, associated with Mercury.
Acmsicu		
Ahmbicv	GD	
a-cocasahe*	AC:C	= *a cocasb*, the time.
Acps		angel, companion of *Psac*.
Acrar		angel, also known as *Acar*.
acroodzi	a-cro-od-zi	beginning. Also *croodzi*. Cf. *iaod, iaodaf*.
acaro odazodi	AC:C	
Acuca		angel, also known as *Acca*.
Acups		angel, also known as *Acps*.
Aczinor		Senior of Earth, associated with Jupiter.
ad	AC:G	See *adrpan*, cast down.
adagita	AC:C	= *adgt*, can.
adana	AC:C, G	= *adna*, obedience.
adapehaheta	AC:C, G	= *adphaht*, unspeakable.

adarepanu	AC: C, G	= *adrpan*, cast down.
adarepeheta	AC: VV	
adarocahe	AC: C	= *adroch*, Mount of Olives.
adgmach		much glory.
adgt	ajt	can, be able.
adagita	AC: C	
Adi		cacodemon, counterpart of the angel *Diom*.
Adire		angel, also known as *Adre*.
adna	ad-na	obedience.
adana	AC: C, G	
Adnop		angel, also known as *Adop*.
Adoeoct		Senior of Fire, associated with Jupiter.
Adoeoet		
adohi*	GD	See *loadohi*, kingdom.
adoho*	AC: C	
adoian	a-do-yan	face.
adoianu	AC: C, G	
adoranu*	AC: G	
Adois		Demonic name (reversal of *Sioda*) commanding cacodemons of Earth of Fire.
Adop		angel, companion of *Dopa*.
Adopa		angel ruling *Dopa* and companions.
adoranu*	AC: G	= *adoian*, face.
Adota		angel also known as *Adta*.
adph	GD	See *piadph*, jaw.
adphaht	ad-fāt	unspeakable.
adapehaheta	AC: C, G	

Adraman		name of an evil spirit.
Adre		angel ruled by *Rzionr Nrzfm*.
Ah-deh-er-reh	GD	Also *Adire*.
Ah-deh-reh	GD	
adroch	ad-roch	Mount of Olives.
adarocahe	AC: C	
adrpan	ad-r-pan	cast down.
adarepanu	AC: C	
adarepeheta	AC: VV	
ad peranuta	AC: G	
Adta		angel, companion of *Taad*.
Advorpt		Governor of the Third Division of the Aethyr *Tex*.
Aetpio		= *Aaetpio*, Senior of Fire.
AF		19.
afa	AC: C	
affa	a-fa	empty.
afafa	AC: G, VV	
afefa	AC: C	
Aflafben		Dee's good angel, appeared to Dee and Kelley on 1 November 1583.
Aphlafben		
ag	ag	none, no, no one.
agi	AC: C	
Agb		cacodemon, counterpart of the angel *Gbal*.
Aglm		angel, companion of *Magl*.
Agmlm		
Ahaozpi		Senior of Air, associated with Venus. Also *Haozpi*.
Ah-deh-er-reh	GD	= *Adre*, angel.
Ah-deh-reh	GD	

Ah-ee-ah-oh-ah-ee		= *Aiaoai,* Divine Name.
Ahmbicv	GD	= *Acmbicu,* Senior of Air.
Aiaoai		Divine Name of Six Letters, ruling Earth of Air.
Aidrom		= *Laidrom,* Senior of Earth.
Aira **Aigra**		Angel skilled in medicine, ruled by *Angpoi Unnax.*
aisaro	AC: C	= *a isro,* the promise.
aji-la-tore-torenu	AC: C	= *ag l toltorn,* no one creature.
ajitoltorenu	AC: C	= *ag toltorn,* no creature.
akarinu	AC: G	praiseworthy. Cf. *ecrin, oecrimi.*
Akele		angel (Filia Lucis), associated with Mars.
aladi	AC: VV, C	= *aldi,* gathering.
aladonu	AC: C, G	= *aldon,* gather.
alalare	AC: C	= *allar,* bind up.
alar **alre**	a-lar AC: C	settle.
alca		judgment(?)
ald*	GD	= *sald,* wonder.
aldaraia		will of God (?) (Another title of the *Book of Soyga.*)
aldi **aladi**	al-di AC: VV, C	gathering. Cf. *aldon.*
aldon **aladonu**	al-don AC: C, G	gather, gird up. Cf. *aldi.*
Alhctga **Alhectega**	 AC: C	Senior of Earth, associated with Venus.

allar	a-lar	bind up.
alalare	AC:C	
Aloai		Divine Name of Five Letters, ruling Fire of Air.
alonusahi	AC:G	= *lonshi,* power.
Alpudus		angelic King ruling in the West-South-West.
alre	AC:C	= *alar,* settle.
am	GD	See *amizpi,* fasten.
amayo*	AC:G	= *enay,* lord.
Ambriol		Governor of the Third Division of the Aethyr *Loe.*
Ambrial		
a-me-ipezodi	AC:C	= *amizpi,* fasten.
amema	AC:C, G	= *amma,* curse.
ametajisa	AC:G	= *emetgis,* seal.
amgedpha		I begin anew.
amizpi	a-miz-pi	fasten.
a-me-ipezodi	AC:C	
am pizi	GD	
amiran	a-mi-ran	yourselves.
amiranu	AC:C, G	
amma	a-ma	curse, cursed.
amema	AC:C, G	
Amox		angel skilled in finding metals and precious stones, ruled by *Vadali Obava.*
Amsox		
An		angel (Filus Filiorum Lucis), associated with Luna.
Aw*	AC:C	
Anaa		angel powerful in change of place, ruled by the angel

		Aanaa and *Vadali Obava*. Also *Anvaa*. Companions are *Naaa, Aaan, Aana*.
Anaeem		Divine Name of Six Letters, ruling Water of Earth.
ananael	a-na-na-el	wisdom.
Ancro		angel also known as *Anro*.
And		cacodemon, counterpart of the angel *Ndzn*.
Andispi		Governor of the Third Division of the Aethyr *Zom*.
aneta-na*	AC:C	=*a netab,* in government.
angelard	an-je-lard	thought, thoughts.
anugelareda	AC:G	
anujelareda	AC:C	
Angpoi		Divine Name of Six Letters, ruling Air of Earth.
Anodoin		Senior of Fire, associated with Mercury.
Anro		angel, companion of *Roan*. Also *Ancro*.
anugelareda	AC:G	=*angelard,* thought.
anujelareda	AC:C	
Anvaa		angel, also known as *Anaa*.
aoiveae	a-oi-ve-ai	star, stars.
Aomi		angel, companion of *Iaom*. Also *Aosmi*.
Aor		cacodemon, counterpart of the angel *Ormn*.
Aosmi		angel, also known as *Aomi*.

Aourrz		Divine Name of Six Letters, ruling Fire of Air.
Aozpi		Holy Name of Five Letters, ruling the element of Air.
Apa		cacodemon, counterpart of the angel *Paoc*.
apachana		'the slimy things made of dust'.
Apahr		angel, also known as *Aphr*.
Apata		demonic name (reversal of *Atapa*) commanding cacodemons of Fire of Water.
Apdoce		=*Aapdoce,* Senior of Fire.
apeta*	AC:G	see *aspt,* before.
Aphlafben		=*Aflafben,* Dee's good angel, appeared to Dee and Kelly on 1 November 1583.
Aphr		angel, companion of *Phra*.
apila	a-pi-la	live (v.)
Aplst		angel, also known as *Apst*.
Apm		cacodemon, counterpart of the angel *Pmox*.
Apst		angel ruled by *Noalmr Oloag*. Also *Aplst*.
aqlo	GD	=*a q loadohi,* in thy kingdom.
aqoso	AC:C	
ar	ar	1) winnow, van. 2) that, so that.
Arbiz		Divine Name of Five Letters, ruling Earth of Earth.

ar-caosaji	AC:C	= *ar caosgi,* winnow the earth.
Ardza		Divine Name of Five Letters, ruling Air of Air.
arecoazodiore	AC:C	= *ar coazior,* that increase.
aretabasa	AC:G	= *ar tabas,* that govern.
are-zodi*	AC:G	= *etharzi,* peace.
Arfaolg		angelic King ruling in the North-North-East.
argedco		(meaning unknown; invoke?)
Arinnap		Senior of Fire, associated with Saturn.
Arizl		angel, also known as *Arzl.*
Arn		name of the Second Aethyr.
arp		conquer? See *zilodarp.*
arphe		descend.
Arsl **Arsel**		Holy Name of Four Letters, ruling the element of Water.
artebasa*	AC:G	= *ar tabas,* that govern.
Arzl		angel, companion of *Rzla.*
Arzulgh		name of an evil spirit, counterpart of *Befafes.*
as **asa**	as AC:C, G	was
asage	AC:G	= *as ge,* was not.
asa-momare	AC:C	= *as momar,* was (and shall be) crowned.
asapata **asapeta**	AC:G AC:C, G	= *aspt,* before.
asata	AC:G	= *as ta,* was as.

Ascha		God.
Ash		cacodemon, counterpart of the angel *Shal.*
Asi		cacodemon, counterpart of the angel *Sisp.*
Asndood		Senior of Fire, associated with Luna.
Asp		name of the Twenty-First Aethyr.
aspian	as-pi-an	quality, qualities.
Aspiaon		Governor of the Third Division of the Aethyr *Deo.*
aspt		before, in front of.
asapata	AC: G	
asapeta	AC: C, G	
as apeta*	AC: G	
Ast		cacodemon, counterpart of the angel *Stim.*
astel		(meaning unknown).
asymp	GD	= *a symp,* with another.
Ataad		angel ruling *Taad* and companions.
Atapa		Divine Name of Five Letters, ruling Fire of Water.
ataraahe	AC: C	= *atraah,* girdle.
Atdim		angel ruling *Tdim* and companions.
Ath		angel (Filia Filiarum Lucis) associated with Venus.
Ato		cacodemon, counterpart of the angel *Tott.*

Atogbo		demonic name (reversal of *Obgota*) commanding cacodemons of Air of Water.
atraah **ataraahe**	a-traa AC:C	girdle, girdles.
auauago	AC:C	=*avavago,* thunder.
auauotza	AC:C	=*avavox,* pomp.
audcal		gold, philosophical mercury.
Audropl		=*Aydropl,* Governor.
Autp **Aultp**		angel, companion of *Utpa.*
Ava		cacodemon, counterpart of the angel *Vasa.*
avabh	a-vab	hyacinth, hyacinthine.
Avabo		demonic name (reversal of *Obava*) commanding cacodemons of Water of Fire.
avavago **auauago**	a-va-va-go AC:C	thunder, thunders. Cf. *coraxo.*
avavox **auauotza**	a-va-vox AC:C	pomp.
Ave		angel (Filius Filiorum Lucis), associated with Venus.
aviny **avini**	a-vi-ni AC:C	millstone, millstones.
Avtotar		Senior of Air, associated with Mercury.
Aw*	AC:C	=*An,* angel.
Axir **Axtir**		angel powerful in transformation, ruled by *Cbalpt Arbiz.*

Axziarg		Governor of the Second Division of the Aethyr *Pax*.
Aydropl **Aydropt** **Audropl**		Governor of the Second Division of the Aethyr *Tan*.
Azcall		demonic name (reversal of *Llacza*) commanding cacodemons of Water of Air.
Azdobn		angel (Filia Lucis), associated with Mercury.
Azdra		demonic name (reversal of *Ardza*) commanding cacodemons of Air of Air.
aziagiar **azodiajiere**	a-zi-a-jar AC:C	harvest.
aziazor **azodiazodore**	a-zi-a-zor AC:C, G	likeness.
Aziz		angel, companion of *Ziza*. Also *Azriz*.
azodiajiere	AC:C	= *aziagiar*, harvest.
azodiazodore	AC:C, G	= *aziazor*, likeness.
azodien	AC:C	= *a zien*, on hands.
Azriz		angel, also known as *Aziz*.

B Pa

Word	Pronunciation / Source	Meaning
Baataiva*		=*Bataiva,* Elemental King of Water.
bab		power, ability, possibility.
babage	ba-ba-je	south.
babagen	ba-ba-jen	
babaje	AC: C, G	
babajehe	AC: C	
babalanuda*	AC: C	=*babalond,* harlot.
Babalel		King, associated with Mars.
babalon	ba-ba-lon	wicked. Cf. *babalond.*
babalonu	AC: C, G	
babalond	ba-ba-lond	harlot. Cf. *babalon.*
babalanuda*	AC: C	
Bablibo		Prince, associated with Sol.
Baeovib	ba-e-o-vib	righteousness; one of the names of God. Cf. *baltoh.*
Baeouib	GD	
Baeouibe	AC: C	
Bag		name of the Twenty-Eighth Aethyr.
Bagenol		Prince, associated with Venus.
bagie	ba-gi-e	fury.
baghie	GD	
bajihie	AC: C	
bagle	bag-le	because, for that reason; why, for what reason?
baglen	bag-len	
bagile	AC: C	
bagilenu	AC: C, G	
bajile	AC: C	
bajileim*	AC: G	

bajilenu	AC:C, G	
bajirele*	AC:C	
Bagledf		Prince, associated with Luna.
bahal	ba-hal	cry aloud.
bahala	AC:C	
bajihie	AC:C	= *bagie,* fury.
bajile	AC:C	= *bagle,* because.
bajileim*	AC:G	= *baglen,* because.
bajilenu	AC:C, G	
bajirele*	AC:C	
balata	AC:C, G	= *balt,* justice.
balatanu	AC:C	= *baltan,* justice.
balatime	AC:G	= *baltim,* justice.
bala-tima	AC:C	
balatoha	AC:C	= *baltoh,* righteousness.
balatohe	AC:C	
balatune*	AC:G	= *baltim,* justice.
balazodareji	AC:G	= *balzarg,* steward.
Balceor		Prince, associated with Saturn.
Baldago		Prince, associated with Jupiter.
balie	GD, AC:C	= *balye,* salt.
Baligon		King, associated with Venus.
balit		just, righteous. Cf. *balt.*
balita	AC:C	
balozodareji	AC:G	= *balzarg,* steward.
balt	balt	justice. Cf. *balit, baltim, baltoh, balzizras.*
balata	AC:C, G	
baltan	bal-tan	
balatanu	AC:C	

baltim	bal-tim	justice, extreme justice.
balatime	AC:G	
bala-tima	AC:C	
balatune*	AC:G	
baltoh	bal-to	righteousness. Cf. *balt, Baeovib.*
balatoha	AC:C	
balatohe	AC:C	
baltoha	AC:C	
balye	bal-ye	salt.
balie	AC:VV, AC:C	
balzarg	bal-zarg	steward.
balazodareji	AC:G	
balzizras	bal-ziz-ras	judgment. Cf. *balt.*
balzodizodarasa	AC:C	
Bamasan		name of a guardian angel.
bamesa	AC:G	= *bams,* forget.
Bamnode		Prince, associated with Saturn.
bams	bams	forget.
bamesa	AC:G	
Bapnido		Prince, associated with Mars.
Barfort		Prince, associated with Mercury.
Bariges		Prince, associated with Sol.
barinu	AC:C	= *brin,* have.
Barma		name of a demon.
Barman		
Barnafa		Prince, associated with Sol.
Bartiro		Prince, associated with Jupiter.
basada*	AC:G	= *busd,* glory.

basajime	AC:C, G	=*basgim*, day.
basajinu*	AC:G	
basgim	bas-jim	day. Cf. *bazm.*
basajime	AC:C, G	
basajinu*	AC:G	
besajinu*	AC:G	
Basmelo		Prince associated with Jupiter. Cf. *bazm?*
Baspalo		Prince, associated with Luna.
Bataivah **Bataivh** **Bataiva** **Baataiva***		Elemental King of Air, associated with Sol.
Bazchim		Governor of the Third Division of the Aethyr *Des.*
bazm	baz-m	midday, noon. Cf. *basgim, basmelo?*
bazodemelo	AC:C	
Bazpama		Prince, associated with Mercury.
Bbemo		demonic name (reversal of *Omebb)* commanding cacodemons of Water of Water.
Befafes		Prince, associated with Mars. Cf. *Befes.* (His name means 'Light from Light').
Befes		(vocative case of) *Befafes,* Prince.
beh-ee-teh-oo-em	GD	=*Bitom,* spirit of Fire.
beh-ee-to-em	GD	
Beigia		angel (Filius Lucis), associated with Mercury.

belanusa	AC:C	=*blans,* harbour.
beliora	AC:C, G	=*bliora,* comfort.
belioraxa	AC:C	=*bliorax,* comfort.
beliore	AC:C	=*blior,* comfort.
beliorebe	AC:C	=*bliorb,* comfort.
beliorese	AC:C	=*bliors,* comfort.
belioreta	AC:C	=*bliort,* comfort.
Belmagel		Kelley's evil angel.
Belmara		Prince, associated with Luna.
Ben		angel who appeared to Dee and Kelley.
Benpagi		Prince, associated with Venus.
berameji	AC:C	=*abramg,* prepare.
beramiji	AC:C	=*abramig,* prepare.
beranusaji	AC:C	=*bransg,* guard.
beregida	AC:C	=*brgda,* sleep.
berinu	AC:C	=*brin,* have.
berinuta	AC:C	=*brint,* have.
berinutasa	AC:C	=*brints,* have.
be-ri-ta	AC:C	=*brita,* talk.
Bermale		Prince, associated with Sol.
Bernole		Prince, associated with Venus.
besajinu*	AC:G	=*basgim,* day.
Besgeme		Prince, associated with Jupiter.

bia	bi-a	voice, voices.
bial	bi-al	
bien	bi-en	
bialo	GD	
bianu	AC:G	
bienu	AC:C	
biab	bi-ab	stand.
biabe	AC:C	
bigliad	big-li-ad	comforter. Cf. *blior, bliorax.*
bijil-iad	AC:C	
Binodab		Prince, associated with Venus.
Binofom		Prince, associated with Mars.
Bitom		spirit of Fire.
beh-ee-teh-oo-em	GD	
beh-ee-to-em	GD	
Blamapo		Prince, associated with Mercury.
blans	blans	harbour, protect, shelter. Cf. *bransg.*
belanusa	AC:C	
bliar		= *blior,* comfort.
bliard		= *bliord,* comfort.
Bliigan		Prince, associated with Mercury.
Blingef		Prince, associated with Jupiter.
Blintom		Prince, associated with Saturn.
blior	bli-or	comfort (n.) Cf. *bliorax.*
bliar	bli-ar	
bliard	bli-ard	
bliora	bli-or-a	

bliorb	bli-orb	
bliors	bli-ors	
bliort	bli-ort	
beliore	AC:C	
beliora	AC:C, G	
beliorebe	AC:C	
beliorese	AC:C	
belioreta	AC:C	
bliorax	bli-or-ax	comfort (v.) Cf. *blior.*
belioraxa	AC:C	
Blisdon		Prince, associated with Mercury.
Blumaza		King, associated with Luna.
Blmaza*		
Bmamgal		Prince, associated with Saturn.
Bmilges		Prince, associated with Mars.
Bminpol		Prince, associated with Mars.
Bnagole		Prince, associated with Venus.
Bnapsen		King, associated with Saturn.
Bnaspol		King, associated with Mercury.
boaluahe	AC:G	worship.
Boaza		angel, also known as *Boza.*
bobanu*	AC:G	=*soboln,* west.
Bobogel		King, associated with Sol.
Bobagel	GD	
Bogemo		(meaning unknown).
bogpa	bog-pa	reign, rule. Cf. *sonf.*
bogira	AC:C	

bojira	AC:G	
bojua	AC:G	
bolanu	AC:G	=*soboln,* west.
bolp	bolp	be! be thou!
bolape	AC:G, C	
Bonefom		Prince, associated with Venus.
booapis	bo-a-pis	serve. Cf. *aboapri.*
booapisa	AC:C	
Bormila		Prince, associated with Venus.
Bornogo		Prince, associated with Sol.
Boza		angel powerful in mixtures of natures, ruled by the angel *Eboza* and *Angpoi Unnax.* Also *Boaza.* Companions are *Ozab, Zabo, Aboz.*
Bracn		angel, also known as *Brcn.*
Bragiop		Prince, associated with Luna.
Bralges		Prince, associated with Luna.
Brasges		
Branglo		Prince, associated with Saturn.
bransg	branzj	guard. Cf. *blans.*
beranusaji	AC:C	
Brap		angel skilled in finding metals and precious stones, ruled by *Vadali Obava.* Also *Briap.*
Brasges		=*Bralges,* Prince.
Brcn		angel, companion of *Cnbr.* Also *Bracn.*

brgda	bërj-da	sleep.
brgdo	GD	
beregida	AC:C	
Briap		angel, also known as *Brap*.
brin	brin	have (they have, you have, thou hast).
brint	brint	
brints	brints	
berinu	AC:C	
berinuta	AC:C	
berinutasa	AC:C	
Brisfli		Prince, associated with Luna.
brita	brita	talk.
be-ri-ta	AC:C	
Brorges		Prince, associated with Saturn.
bufd*		= *busd*, glory.
busada	AC:C, G	= *busd*, glory.
busadire	AC:C	= *busdir*, glory.
busd	buzd	glory.
busdir	buz-dir	
bufd*		
busada	AC:C	
basada*	AC:G	
busadire	AC:C	
Busduna		Prince, associated with Mars.
butmon	but-mon	mouth, mouths.
butmona	but-mo-na	
butmoni	but-mo-ni	
butamonu	AC:C	
butamona	AC:C	
butamoni	AC:C	
Butmono		Prince, associated with Saturn.
Bynepor		King, associated with Jupiter.

C/K Veh

c	s	1) on, with, of, unto. 2) o, oh.
ca **eca** **eka**	ka AC:C, G; GD GD	1) therefore. 2) as. Cf. *ta*. 3) another. Cf. *symp*.
cab **caba**	kab AC:C	rod.
Cab		cacodemon, counterpart of the angel *Abmo*.
caba	ka-ba	govern. (More usually *taba)*.
Cabalpt		= *cbalpt*, Divine Name.
Cac		cacodemon, counterpart of the angel *Acca*.
cacacom **ca-ca-come**	ka-ka-kom AC:C	flourish.
cacocasb **cacocasabe**	AC:C AC:C	= *ca cocasb*, another time.
cacrg **cacareji** **kakareji** **kakoreji** **cacureji**	ka-kërj AC:C AC:G AC:G AC:C	until.
Cadaamp		angelic King ruling in the North-North-West.
caelazod	AC:C, G	= *calz*, firmament.
cafafam **cafafame**	ka-fa-fam AC:C	abiding, abode.
caharisateosa	AC:C	= *christeos*, let there be.
cahirelanu	AC:C	= *chirlan*, rejoice.

cahisa	AC:C, G	= *chis,* are.
kahisa	AC:G	
cahisaji	AC:C	= *chis ge,* are not.
cahiso	AC:C	= *chiso,* are.
cala	AC:C	= *CLA,* 456.
calaa	AC:C	
calz	kalz	firmament.
caelazod	AC:C	
Calzirg		Governor of the Third Division of the Aethyr *Lin.*
Cam		cacodemon, counterpart of the angel *Amox.*
camascheth		(meaning unknown).
cameliatza	AC:G	= *camliax,* speak.
cameliaxa	AC:C	
camikas		(meaning unknown).
camliax	kam-li-ax	speak, spake.
cameliatza	AC:G	
cameliaxa	AC:C	
canal	ka-nal	workman, workmen.
canale	AC:C	
kanila	AC:G	= *cnila,* blood.
canilu	AC:C	
ca-ni-quola*	AC:C	= *c noqod, c noqodi,* o you servants.
ca-ni-quodi	AC:C	
ca-no-quoda	AC:C, G	
canse		mighty. Cf. *cruscanse.*
ca-ol	AC:G	meaning unknown; perhaps *ca,* therefore.
caosg	ka-ozg	earth.
caosga	ka-oz-ga	

caosgi	ka-oz-ji	
caosgin	ka-oz-jin	
caosgo	ka-oz-go	
caosgon	ka-oz-gon	
caosaga	AC:C, G	
caosagi	AC:C, G	
caosaji	AC:C, G	
caosajinu	AC:C	
caosago	AC:C, G	
caosagonu	AC:C	
coasg*	GD	
capimali	ka-pi-ma-li	successively, time after time.
capmiali	kap-mi-a-li	
cape-mi-ali	AC:C	
capimao	ka-pi-ma-o	time, period, season, while.
capimaon	ka-pi-ma-on	
carbaf	kar-baf	sink.
carebafe	AC:C	
carep-el	AC:C	=*crp l,* but one.
caresa*	AC:C	=*cors,* such.
caripe	AC:C	=*crip,* but.
carma		come out. Cf. *niis.*
Carmara		angelic King ruling the Kings and Princes of the planetary hours. Also called Marmara.
caro-o-dazodi	AC:C	=*croodzi,* beginning.
casarm	ka-sarm	whom, in whom, to whom, under whom, of whom, whose. Cf. *ds.*
casarma	ka-sar-ma	
casarman	ka-sar-man	
casarmg	ka-sarmj	
casarmi	ka-sar-mi	
casarem	AC:C	
casareme	AC:C, G	
kasareme	AC:G	

casarema	AC:C	
casaremanu	AC:C	
casaremeji	AC:C	
kasaremeji	AC:G	
casaremi	AC:C	
catabela	AC:C	=*orsca tbl,* the buildings of her.
cbalpt		Divine Name of Six Letters, ruling Earth of Earth.
cabalpt		
kelpadman		(meaning unknown).
ceph		name of the Enochian letter representing Z.
cheph		
keph		
Chialps		Governor of the Second Division of the Aethyr *Nia.*
chiis	kis	are. Cf. *chis.*
childao	kil-da-o	diamond, diamonds.
chirlan	kir-lan	rejoice.
cahirelanu	AC:C	
Chirspa		Governor of the First Division of the Aethyr *Asp.*
chis	kis	are (they are).
chiis	kis	
chiso	ki-so	
cahisa	AC:C, G	
kahisa	AC:G	
cahiso	AC:C	
chisa	GD	=*chis a,* are in.
Choronzon	AC:VV	=*Coronzon,* demon.
Chr		name of the Twentieth Aethyr.
Khr	AC:C	
chramsa		(meaning unknown).

christeos	kris-te-os	let there be.
caharisateosa	AC:C	
ci	AC:C	see *ulcinin,* happy.
CIAL		9996.
ciaofi	si-a-o-fi	terror.
ciaosi	AC:C	
kiaisi*	AC:G	
cicle	si-kle	mystery, mysteries.
cicles	si-kles	
cicale	AC:C	
kikale	AC:G, GD	
kikle	GD	
cicalesa	AC:C	
cinxir	GD	=*cynxir,* mingle.
CLA		456.
Cms		cacodemon, counterpart of the angel *Msal.*
Cnbr		angel powerful in mechanical arts, ruled by *Aiaoai Oiiit* and the angel *Hcnbr.* Companions are *Nbrc, Brcn, Rcnb.*
Cnabr		
cnila	kni-la	blood.
kanila	AC:G	
canilu	AC:C	
c-noqol	GD	=*c noqod,* o you servants.
coasg*	GD	=*caosg,* earth.
coazior	ko-a-zi-or	increase.
coazodiore	AC:C	
Cocarpt	AC:C	=*Cucarpt,* Governor.
cocasb	ko-kazb	time, times.
cocasg	ko-kazj	
cocasa	AC:C	

kokasa	AC:G	
cocasabe	AC:C	
cocasaji	AC:C	
a-cocasahe*	AC:C	
collal	ko-lal	sleeve, sleeves.
colalala	AC:C	
Comanan		Governor of the Second
Comananu	GD	Division of the Aethyr *Zax*.
comerelahe*	AC:G	= *comselh,* circle.
commah	ko-ma	truss, trussed.
comemahe	AC:C	
commemahe	AC:G	
commennahe*	AC:G	
como	ko-mo	window.
comselh	kom-sel	circle.
com-selahe	AC:C	
comselha	AC:C	
komesalehe	AC:G	
komesalahe	AC:G	
komesalohe	AC:G	
komeselake*	AC:G	
komeselahe	AC:G	
kromeselahe*	AC:G	
congamphlgh		man's spirit; the Holy Ghost.
conisa*	AC:C	= *eolis,* make.
conisbra	ko-niz-bra	works of man.
conisabera	AC:C	
const	konst	thunder. Cf. *avavago, coraxo.*
conusata	AC:C	
Cop		cacodemon, counterpart of the angel *Opna*.
copehanu*	AC:C	= *eophan,* lamentation.

cor	kor	number. Cf. *cormf, cormp.*
core	AC:C	
Corabiel		planetary angel presiding over the sphere of Mercury.
coraxo	ko-rax-o	thunder. Cf. *const, avavago.*
cordziz	kord-ziz	reasonable creature, man (Homo sapiens).
coredazodizoda	AC:C	
koredazodizod	AC:G	
Corfax		name of a guardian angel.
cormf	kormf	number. Cf. *cor, cormp.*
cormfa	korm-fa	
coremefa	AC:C, G	
cormp	kormp	number (v.), count, be numbered.
cormpo	korm-po	
cormpt	kormpt	
coremepe	AC:C	
coremepo	AC:C	
coremepeta	AC:C	
Coronzon		name of a mighty demon (perhaps = Lucifer) who rebelled against God.
Coronzom		
Choronzon	AC:VV	
cors	kors	such.
coresa	AC:C	
coresi*	AC:C	
corsi*	GD	
caresa*	AC:C	
Cpsa		angel, companion of *Psac.*
Cpusa		
Cralpir		Governor of the Second Division of the Aethyr *Zip.*
crip	krip	but, only.
crp	krip	
caripe	AC:C	

croodzi	kro-od-zi	beginning. Also *acroodzi*. Cf. *iaod, iaodaf*.
kromeselahe*	AC:G	= *comselh*, circle.
cruscanse		more mighty. Cf. *canse*.
Csc		cacodemon, counterpart of the angel *Scio*.
Cucarpt		Governor of the First Division of the Aethyr *Lea*.
Cocarpt	AC:C	
kures		here (?)
Cus		cacodemon, counterpart of the angel *Ussn*.
cynxir	sinx-ir	mingle, mingled; mix, mixed.
cinxir	GD	
cynuxire	AC:C	
kynutzire	AC:G	
Czns		angel ruled by *Idoigo Ardza*.
Czons		
Czodenes		

D Gal

d	di	three, third.
da	AC:C	
dau	AC:C	
da	da	1) there.
	AC:C	2) = *d,* three.
Daalo		demonic name (reversal of *Olaad,* commanding cacodemons of Earth of Water.
dalagare	AC:C	= *dlugar,* give.
Daltt		angel also known as *Datt.*
daluga	AC:C, G	= *dluga,* give.
dalugare	AC:C	= *dlugar,* give.
damploz	dam-ploz	variety.
damepelozoda	AC:C	
dao	AC:C	See *childao,* diamond.
DAOX		5678
Dapi		angel ruled by *Iaaasd Atapa.* Also *Daspi.*
darbs	darbz	obey.
darebesa	AC:C, G	
dare-pasa*	AC:G	
dorebasa*	AC:G	
dorebesa*	AC:G	
dorepesa*	AC:G	
dareji	AC:C	= *DARG,* 6739.
daresare	AC:C	= *darsar,* wherefore.
DARG		6739.
dareji	AC:C	

darilapa	AC:C	= *drilpa,* great.
darisapa*	AC:C, G	
darilapi	AC:C	= *drilpi,* great.
darix	AC:C	= *drix,* bring down.
darolanu	AC:C	= *droln,* any.
darr		the philosopher's stone.
darsar	dar-sar	wherefore. Cf. *bagle.*
daresare	AC:C	
das	AC:C, G	= *ds,* which.
dasata	AC:C	= *ds t,* which also.
dasonuf	AC:C	= *ds sonf,* which reign.
Daspi		angel also known as *Dapi.*
Datt		angel powerful in transformation, ruled by *Volxdo Sioda.*
dau	AC:G	= *d,* three.
dax	dax	loin, loins.
dazis	da-zis	head, heads.
dazodisa	AC:C	
de	di	of, to.
dedvilh		(meaning unknown).
Deo		name of the Seventh Aethyr.
Des		name of the Twenty-Sixth Aethyr.
desa*	AC:C	= *od es,* and fourth.
Dial		Holy Name of Four Letters, ruling the Element of Earth.
dial*	AC:C	= *d ialprt,* third flame.

Dialiva		Governor of the Third Division of the Aethyr *Arn*.
Diari		angel also known as *Diri*.
dilzmo	dilz-mo	differ.
dizodalamo*	AC:C	
Dimt		angel, companion of *Tdim*.
Dinmt		
Diom		angel powerful in transformation, ruled by *Volxdo Sioda*. Also *Dixom*.
Diri		angel skilled in finding metals and precious stones, ruled by *Llacza Palam*. Also *Diari*.
diu	di-u	angle.
di-vau	AC:C	
duiv	GD	
Dixom		angel also known as *Diom*.
dizodalamo*	AC:C	= *dilzmo*, differ.
dlasod		sulphur (alchemical). Cf. *salbrox*.
dluga	dlu-ga	give, given.
dlugam	dlu-gam	
dlugar	dlu-gar	
daluga	AC:C, G	
dalugare	AC:C	
Dmal		angel (Filius Lucis) associated with Jupiter.
do	AC:G	in.
Doagnis		Governor of the First Division of the Aethyr *Arn*.
doalim	do-a-lim	sin (v.)
doalime	AC:C	

Doanzin		Governor of the Third Division of the Aethyr *Zip*.
dobix	do-bix	fall.
dobitza	AC:C	
Docepax		Governor of the Third Division of the Aethyr *Zim*.
dodapala	AC:C	= *dodpal,* vex.
dodaremeni	AC:C	= *dodrmni,* vex.
dodasa	AC:C	= *dods,* vexation.
dodasihe	AC:C	= *dodsih,* vexation.
dodpal	dod-pal	vex. Cf. *dodsih.*
dodrmni	dod-ërm-ni	
dods	dodz	
dodapala	AC:C	
dodaremeni	AC:C	
dodasa	AC:C	
dodsih	dod-si	vexation. Cf. *dodpal.*
dodseh	GD	
Dolop		angel also known as *Doop*.
don		name of the Enochian letter representing R.
donasdogamatastos		hell-fire.
Donpa		angel also known as *Dopa*.
dooain	do-o-ain	name.
dooaip	do-o-aip	
dooiap	do-o-yap	
dooainu	AC:C, G	
dooaipe	AC:C, G	
dooiape	AC:C, G	
doooape*	AC:G	

Doop		angel powerful in transformation, ruled by *Cbalpt Arbiz*. Also *Dolop*.
Dopa		angel powerful in mixtures of natures, ruled by *Noalmr Oloag* and the angel *Adopa*. Also *Donpa*. Companions are *Opad, Pado, Adop*.
dorebasa*	AC:G	= *darbs*, obey.
dorebesa*	AC:G	
dorepesa*		
dorpha	dor-fa	look about.
dorphal	dor-fal	
dorepaha	AC:C	
dorepehal	AC:C	
dorepehala	AC:G	
dorepehela	AC:G	
dosig	do-sij	night.
dosiji	AC:C	
Dozinal		Governor of the Fourth Division of the Aethyr *Tex*.
drilpa	dril-pa	great, greater. Cf. *canse*.
drilpi	dril-pi	
darilapa	AC:C	
darilapi	AC:C, G	
darisapa*	AC:C, G	
drix	drix	bring down.
darix	AC:C	
droln	droln	any.
darolanu	AC:C	
drux		name of the Enochian letter representing N.
drun	GD	

ds	di-es	who, which, that. Cf. *casarm.*
Dsaaai		demonic name (reversal of *Iaaasd)* commanding cacodemons of Fire of Water.
Dtaa **Dtoaa**		angel, companion of *Taad.*
duiv	GD	= *diu,* angle.
Dxgz **Dxagz**		angel, companion of *Xgzd.*

E Graph

E		angel (Filia Lucis) associated with Sol.
Eac		cacodemon, counterpart of the angel *Acar*.
eai	e-ai	among, amongst. Cf. *aaf, oai*.
Eboza		angel ruling *Boza* and companions.
eca	AC: C, G; GD	= *ca*, therefore.
Ecop		angel skilled in finding metals and precious stones, ruled by *Vadali Obava*.
Ecaop		
ecrin	e-krin	praise (n.) Cf. *oecrimi*.
ecarinu	AC: C	
e-karinu	AC: G	
akarinu	AC: G	
Edelprna		Elemental King of Fire, associated with Sol.
Edelperna		
Edelprnaa	AC: C	
Edlprnaa	GD	
ednas	ed-nas	visit. Cf. *f*.
eda-nasa	AC: C	
ef	AC: C, GD	= *f*, visit.
efafafe	e-fa-fa-fe	vial, vials. Also *ofafafe*.
efafaje*	AC: C	
efe		(meaning unknown).
eh-ex-ar-peh	GD	= *Exarp*, Spirit of Air.
eka	GD	= *ca*, therefore.
e-karinu	AC: G	= *ecrin*, praise.

Ekiei		angel (Filia Filiarum Lucis) associated with Mars.
El		angel (Filia Lucis) associated with Sol.
el	el	one, first. Also *l.*
ela	AC:C, G	
elanusahe	AC:G	= *lansh,* power.
elanusaha	AC:C	
elasa*	AC:G	= *ils,* you.
elasadi	AC:C	= *lasdi,* foot.
elazodape	AC:G	= *elzap,* course.
Elexarpeh	GD	= *Lexarph,* Governor.
elo	el-o	first. Cf. *el.*
elonu-dohe	AC:G	= *londoh,* kingdom.
elonusa	AC:C, G	= *lonsa,* power.
elonusahi	AC:C, G	= *lonshi,* power.
elonusahinu	AC:C, G	= *lonshin,* power.
elzap	el-zap	course.
elazodape	AC:C, G	
elzodape	AC:G	
em	em	nine. Also *m.*
emena	AC:C	= *emna,* herein.
emetgis	e-met-jis	seal.
ametajisa	AC:G	
emetajisa	AC:C, G	
emna	em-na	herein.
emena	AC:C	
EMOD		8763.
emoda	AC:C	

Emor	GD	=*Mor,* Holy Name.
Empeh	GD	=*Mph,* Holy Name.
En-ah-en-tah	GD	=*Nanta,* Spirit of Earth.
Enai	AC:C	=*Enay,* Lord.
E-na-iad	AC:C	=*Enay Iad,* Lord God.
Enay	en-e	Lord. Also *Na.*
Enayo	AC:C, G	
eol	e-ol	make, made. Cf. *eolis.*
e-ola	AC:G	
eolis	e-o-lis	making. Cf. *eol.*
eophan	e-o-fan	lamentation. Cf. *ser.*
copehanu*	AC:C	
eors	e-ors	hundred.
eoresa	AC:C	
Ephra		angel ruling *Phra* and companions.
ERAN		6332.
Eranu	AC:C	
erem	AC:C	=*erm,* ark.
Erg		cacodemon, counterpart of the angel *Rgan.*
erm	erm	ark.
erem	AC:C	
Ern		cacodemon, counterpart of the angel *Rnil.*
es	es	four. Also *s.*
Erzla		angel ruling *Rzla* and companions.
Ese		angel (Filia Lucis) associated with Venus.

Esemeli		angel (Filia Filiarum Lucis) associated with Saturn.
esiasch	e-si-ask	brother, brothers.
esiasacahe	AC:C, G	
siasch	GD	
ethamz	e-thamz	cover (v.).
etahamezoda	AC:C	
ethamza	GD	
etharzi	e-thar-zi	peace.
Eutpa		angel ruling *Utpa* and companions.
ex	AC:C	see *oxex,* vomit.
Exarp		Spirit of Air.
Exentaser	AC:VV	Mother of All (?).
Exr		cacodemon, counterpart of the angel *Xrnh.*

F Or

f	ef	visit. Also *ef.*
fa	AC:C	
fe	AC:G	
faaip	fa-a-ip	voice, voices. Cf. *bia.*
fa-a-ipe	AC:C	
Faax		angel skilled in medicine, ruled by *Obgota Aabco.* Also *Fatax.*
faboan	fa-bo-an	poison.
faboanu	AC:C, G	
fafen	fa-fen	1) to the intent that.
fafenu	AC:C	2) follower, followers.
fam		name of the Enochian letter representing S.
faoda*	AC:C	=*iaod,* beginning.
faonts	fānts	dwell. Cf. *faorgt, praf.*
faonutas	AC:C	
faorgt	farjt	dwelling-place. Cf. *faonts.*
fargt	farjt	
faoregita	AC:C, G	
faorejita	AC:G	
faregita	AC:C	
farzm	far-zëm	lift up, raise. Cf. *goholor.*
farsm	GD	
farezodem	AC:C	
fatahe-are-zodi	AC:G	=*f etharzi,* visit with peace.
Fatax		angel, also known as *Faax.*
FAXS		7336. More usually TAXS.
faxisa	AC: C	

felathe-are-zodi*	AC:G	=*f etharzi,* visit with peace.
fetahe*	AC:G	
fetahe-ar-ezodi	AC:C	
fetahe-are-zodi	AC:G	
fifalz	fi-falz	weed out.
fifalazoda	AC:C	
fifis	fi-fis	execute, perform, carry out.
fifisa	AC:C	
fisis*	GD	
Fmnd		angel skilled in medicine,
Fmond		ruled by *Idoigo Ardza.*
Focisni		Governor of the Second Division of the Aethyr *Bag.*

g **gi** **ji**	ji ji AC:G	1) with, in. 2) you, your.
GA		31.
Ga		name of an angel who appeared to Dee and Kelley ('Last breath of the living').
gag		(meaning unknown).
gah **gahe**	gā AC:C, G	spirit, spirits.
gaha	AC:VV	1) existed. 2) Babes of the Abyss (?)
gahal	AC:VV	exists.
gahalana	AC:VV	will exist.
gahire		(meaning unknown).
Gahoachma		I am what I am (a title of God).
Gaiol		Holy Name of Five Letters, ruling the Element of Water.
gal		name of the Enochian letter representing D.
galgol		(meaning unknown).
galsuagaph **galsuagath**		(meaning unknown).
Galvah		name of an angel who appeared to Dee and Kelley on 14 June 1583. His name means 'end'.
Ganislay		name of a demon.

ganiurax		(meaning unknown).
Gaolo		demonic name (reversal of *Oloag*) commanding cacodemons of Air of Fire.
garmal		(meaning unknown).
garnastel		(meaning unknown).
garp		(meaning unknown).
gascampho		(meaning unknown: 'the word has 64 significations').
gassagen		'the divine power creating the angel of the same'.
Gazavaa		name formed of the angels *Ga, Za, Vaa.*
Gbal **Gbeal**		angel skilled in finding metals and precious stones, ruled by *Anaeem Sondn (?)*
ge	je	1) not. 2) our.
Gebabal		angelic King ruling in the East-North-East.
Gecaond		Governor of the First Division of the Aethyr *Zim.*
ged		name of the Enochian letter representing G.
Gedoons		Governor of the Second Division of the Aethyr *Loe.*
gedotbar		begotten.
geh	je	thou art.
gemeganza		your will be done.
Gemnimb		Governor of the Second Division of the Aethyr *Tex.*

Genadol		Governor of the Second Division of the Aethyr *Deo*.
genetaahe*	AC:G	=*g netaab*, your government.
gephna		(meaning unknown).
ger		name of the Enochian letter representing Q.
geraa	AC:G	=*graa*, moon.
geta		out of him.
gevamna		beginning (?)
gi		=*g*, with.
gigipah	ji-ji-pa	breath.
gigipahe	AC:C	
jijipahe	AC:G	
gil		we want (?)
jimi-calazodoma	AC:C	=*g micalz oma*, with a power of understanding.
ginai	AC:C	=*gnay*, does.
jinayo	AC:C	
ginetaabe	AC:C	=*g netaab*, your government.
ginonupe	AC:C	=*gnonp*, garnish.
giraa	AC:C	=*graa*, moon.
giresam	AC:C	=*g rsam*, with admiration.
jirosabe	AC:C, G	=*grosb*, sting.
gisg		name of the Enochian letter
gisa	GD	representing T.
Githgulcag		name of a demon (perhaps Lucifer).
givi	ji-vi	stronger. Cf. *drilpa*, *canse*.

gizyax	jiz-yax	earthquake.
jizodajazoda	AC:G	
jizodyazoda	AC:C	
Glma		angel, companion of *Magl.*
Glmma		
glo	GD	see *tofglo,* all things.
Gmnm		angel skilled in finding metals and precious stones, ruled by *Vadali Obava.*
Gmdnm		
gna		(meaning unknown).
gnay	jë-nei	does.
ginai	AC:C	
jinayo	AC:C	
gnetaab	GD	=*g netaab,* your government.
gnonp	jë-nomp	garnish.
ginonupe	AC:C	
go-a-al*	AC:G	=*qaal,* creator.
go-a-anu*	AC:G	=*qaan,* creation.
gohe	go-he	say, saying, said, (he says).
gohia	go-hi-a	(we say).
goho	go-ho	(he says).
gohol	go-hol	(saying).
gohon	go-hon	(have said).
gohulim	go-hu-lim	(it is said to you).
gohus	go-hus	(I say).
gohas	AC:G	
gohola	AC:C, G	
gohu	AC:C	
gohulime	AC:C	
gohusa	AC:C, G	
gohed		one, everlasting.
goholor	go-ho-lor	lift up, raise. Cf. *farzm.*
goholore	AC:C, G	

Gomziam		Governor of the Third Division of the Aethyr *Rii.*
gon		name of the Enochian letter representing I.
gono	go-no	faith.
gonsag		(meaning unknown).
go-o-al*	AC: G	= *qaal,* creator.
gosaa	go-sā	stranger.
graa	grā	moon.
geraa	AC: G	
giraa	AC: C	
gran	gran	elder, elders. Also *uran.*
graph		name of the Enochian letter representing E.
grosb	grozb	sting, bitter sting.
jirosabe	AC: C, G	
gru		deed, fact.
Gzdx		angel, companion of *Xgzd.*
Gzadx		

H Na

ha		(meaning unknown).
Habioro		Senior of Air, associated with Mars. Also *Abioro.*
Hagone		angel (Filius Filiorum Lucis), associated with Mercury; also, the angelic Prince ruling, with King Carmara, the Kings and Princes of the planetary hours.
Hagonel		
hal		(meaning unknown).
hami	ha-mi	creature, creatures.
ham	ham	
Haozpi		=*Ahaozpi,* Senior of Air.
harg	harj	plant (v.)
haraji	AC:C	
Hbr		cacodemon, counterpart of the angel *Brap.*
Hcmorda		=*Htmorda,* Senior of Air.
Hcnbr		angel ruling *Cnbr* and companions.
Hcoma		Spirit of Water.
heh-co-em-ah	GD	
Hctga		Holy Name of Five Letters, ruling the Element of Earth.
Hectega	GD	
he	GD	see *luiahe,* song.
Heeoa		angel (Filius Lucis), associated with Mars.
helech		in ours (?)

Hiaom		angel ruling *Iaom* and companions.
Hipotga		Senior of Air, associated with Saturn.
hoath	ho-ath	worshipper.
hoathahe	AC:C	
hoel-q	AC:C	= *holq*, measure.
holdo	hol-do	groan.
holado	AC:G, C	
holq	holk	measure (v.)
hoel-q	AC:C	
hometohe	AC:C, G	= *homtoh*, triumph.
homin	ho-min	age.
homil	ho-mil	
homida*	AC:C, G	
homila	AC:C, G	
homtoh	hom-to	triumph (v.)
hometohe	AC:C, G	
Hononol		angelic King ruling in the West.
hoxmarch		fear (n.)
Hrap		angel, companion of *Phra*.
Hraap		
Hroan		angel ruling *Roan* and companions.
Hru		cacodemon, counterpart of the angel *Ruoi*.
Hsa		cacodemon, counterpart of the angel *Saiz*.
Htmorda		Senior of Air, associated with Luna.
Hcmorda		

Hua		cacodemon, counterpart of the angel *Vasg.*
hubaio	hu-bay-o	lantern, lamp.
hubar	hu-bar	
hubaro	hu-bar-o	
hubardo	GD	
hubare	AC:C	
hucacha		(meaning unknown).
huseh		(meaning unknown).
Hxgzd		angel ruling *Xgzd* and companions.

I/Y Gon

i	i	1) is. 2) in. 3) angel (Filius Lucis) associated with Sol.
Iaaasd		Divine Name of Six Letters, ruling Fire of Water.
Iaba		angel ruled by *Spmnir Llpiz.* Also *Ianba.*
Iabes		God, Lord; Supreme Life.
Iad	yad	God.
iado		
Iada	AC:C, G	
iadnah	yad-na	knowledge, divine knowledge.
iadnamad	yad-na-mad	
iadanahe	AC:C	
iadanamada	AC:C	
Iadpil	yad-pil	one of the names of God: 'He That Lives'.
Iahl		angel skilled in finding metals and precious stones, ruled by *Anaeem Sondn.* Also *Iamhl.*
iaiadix	ya-ya-dix	honor.
iaial	ya-yal	include (conclude).
Iaida	yai-da	a title of God: 'The Highest'.
Iaidon	yai-don	a title of God: 'The All-Powerful'.
ialapereji	AC:G	= *ialprg,* flame.
iala-pire-gahe	AC:C, G	= *ialpirgah,* flames of first glory.

ialaponu	AC:G	= *ialpon,* burn.
yalaponu	AC:C	
ialapore	AC:C	= *ialpor,* burning.
Yalpamb		Governor of the Third Division of the Aethyr *Zen.*
ialpereji	AC:C	= *ialprg,* flame.
ialpirgah	yal-pir-ga	flames of first glory. Cf. *ialprg.*
iala-pire-gahe	AC:C, G	
ialpirt	GD	= *ialprt,* flame.
ialpon	yal-pon	burn. Cf. *ialpor.*
ialaponu	AC:G	
yalaponu	AC:C	
ialpor	yal-por	burning, flaming.
ialapore	AC:C	
ialprg	yal-përj	flame, flames. Cf. *ialpirgah, vep.*
ialprt	yal-përt	
ialapereji	AC:G	
ialpereji	AC:C	
ialpirt	GD	
Iamhl		angel also known as *Iahl.*
Iana		angel (Filia Lucis) associated with Jupiter.
Ianba		angel also known as *Iaba.*
Iaoaia		demonic name (reversal of *Aiaoai*) commanding cacodemons of Earth of Air.
iaod	ya-od	beginning. Cf. *croodzi.*
iaodaf	ya-o-daf	
yaodafe	AC:C	
Iaola		demonic name (reversal of *Aloai*) commanding cacodemons of Fire of Air.

Iaom **Iasom**		angel powerful in finding out secrets of men, ruled by the angel *Hiaom* and *Spmnir Llpiz*. Companions are *Aomi, Omia, Miao*.
yarry **yareryo**	ya-ri AC:C	providence.
iasa*	AC:C	= *las*, rich.
Ibah		Holy Name of Four Letters, ruling the Element of Air.
i-be-da	AC:G	triangle.
Ich		name of the Eleventh Aethyr.
icoresaka*	AC:C	= *i cors ca*, is such as.
Iczhhcal **Iczhhca** **Iczhhcl** **Iczhhcz** **Iczodhehca**		Elemental King of Earth, associated with Sol.
Idalam		demonic name (reversal of *Maladi*) commanding cacodemons of Earth of Water.
idalugame **idalu-gamea**	AC:G AC:C	= *i dlugam*, is given.
Idoian	AC:VV	Holy Name (name of God).
Idoigo	i-do-i-go	1) a title of God: 'He that sits on the Holy Throne'. 2) Divine Name of Six Letters, ruling Air of Air.
iecarimi*	AC:C	= *oecrimi*, praise.
iehe	AC:C, G	= *geh*, thou art.

iehusoz	ye-hu-soz	mercy.
iehusozod	AC:G	
yehusozod	AC:C	
iehusozoda	AC:G	
i-el	AC:C	=*i l*, is one.
Ih		angel (Filius Lucis), associated with Luna.
Iipo **Iidpo**		angel powerful in transformation, ruled by *Maladi Olaad*.
iisononu*	AC:C	=*lilonon*, branch.
il	il	thou, thee. Also *ils*.
ila	AC:G	
Ilacza		=*Llacza*, Divine Name.
Iladav		demonic name (reversal of *Vadali*) commanding cacodemons of Water of Fire.
ilas	AC:G	=*ils*, thou.
ilasa	AC:C, G	
Ilemese		angel (Filius Filiorum Lucis), associated with Saturn.
ilesa	AC:G	=*ils*, thou.
ili	AC:C	=*i li*, in the first.
ili-i	AC:G	o ye hills.
ilonon	GD	=*lilonon*, branch.
Ilr		angel (Filius Lucis), associated with Venus. Also *Isc*.
ils	ils	thou, thee. Also *il*.
yls	ils	
ylsi	ilsi	

ilas	AC: G	
ilasa	AC: C, G	
ilesa	AC: G	
ilsi	GD	
yolasa	AC: C	
i-mica-ol-zododa*	AC: C	= *omicaolz,* be mighty.
imimuamare*	AC: G	= *imvamar,* apply oneself.
Imtd		angel, companion of *Tdim.*
Imntd		
imvamar	im-va-mar	apply oneself.
imimuamare*	AC: G	
imuamar	AC: C	
imumamare	AC: G	
in	GD	= *m,* except.
inoasa	AC: C	= *i noas,* is become.
insi	in-si	walk.
inusi	AC: C	
Iocle		angel (Filius Filiorum Lucis), associated with Mars.
iod	AC: C	= *i od,* is and.
Ioiad	i-o-yad	a title of God: 'He that Lives Forever'.
Io-iiad	GD	
yolasa	AC: C	= *ils,* thou.
yolcam	yol-kam	bring forth.
yolci	yol-si	
iolcam	GD	
yolacame	AC: C	
yolakame	AC: G	
yolaci	AC: C	
yolaki	AC: G	
Iopgna		demonic name (reversal of *Angpoi*) commanding cacodemons of Air of Earth.

yor	yor	roar.
yorb	GD	
yore	AC:C	
yorepoila	AC:C	=*yrpoil,* division.
ip	ip	not. Cf. *ipam, ipamis.*
ipe	AC:C	
ipam	i-pam	is not. Cf. *ip, ipamis.*
ipame	AC:C, G	
ipamis	i-pa-mis	cannot be. Cf. *ip, ipam.*
ipamisa	AC:G	
iparanu	AC:G	=*ip uran,* not see.
ipuranu	AC:C	
irgil	ir-jil	how many.
irejila	AC:C	
yrpoil	ir-poil	division. Cf. *poilp.*
yorepoila	AC:C	
isa*	AC:G	=*as,* was.
isalamanu	AC:C	=*i salman,* is the house.
isaro	AC:C	=*isro,* promise.
Isc		=*Ilr,* angel.
isro	iz-ro	promise.
isaro	AC:C	
itahila	AC:C	=*othil,* seat.
itzomatzipe	AC:C	=*ixomaxip,* known.
Iubanladaec		name of an angel who appeared to Dee and Kelley on 19 June 1583.
Jubanladaec		
Jubanladaa*		
Jubenladece		
iudra		(meaning unknown).
ivame*	AC:C	=*i umd,* is called.
ivaumed	AC:G	

ivaumeda	AC:G	
ivaunieda	AC:G	
ivemeda	AC:C	
ixomaxip	ix-o-max-ip	known. Cf. *om.*
itzomatzipe	AC:C	
Izaz		angel, companion of *Ziza.* Also *Izraz.*
izazaz	i-za-zaz	frame, framed.
i-zoda-zodazod	AC:C	
Ized		angel (Filia Filiarum Lucis), associated with Jupiter.
Izinr		angel, also known as *Iznr.*
Izixp		angel, also known as *Izxp.*
izizop	i-zi-zop	vessel, vessels; container. Also *zizop.*
izodizodope	AC:C	
Iznr		angel skilled in medicine, ruled by *Angpoi Unnax.* Also *Izinr.*
i-zoda-zodazod	AC:C	= *izazaz,* frame.
izodizodope	AC:C	= *izizop,* vessel.
Izraz		angel, also known as *Izaz.*
Izxp		angel ruled by *Spmnir Llpiz.* Also *Izixp.*

L Ur

L	el	1) one, first; The First (a title of God). Cf. *la, li, lo.*
	AC:C	2) angel (Filius Filiorum Lucis), associated with Sol.
la	la	first. Cf. *l, li, lo.*
Labnixp		Governor of the First Division of the Aethyr *Bag.*
laf		(meaning unknown).
lah		(meaning unknown).
laiad	lai-ad	secret, secrets.
laiada	AC:C, G	
Laidrom		Senior of Earth, associated with Mars. Also *Aidrom.*
Lairz		angel also known as *Larz.*
Lanacon	AC:C	=*Lavacon,* Governor.
Lang		ministering angels.
lanibame	AC:C	=*l nibm,* one season.
lansh	lonsh	power. Also *lonsa, lonshi, lonshin.*
Laoaxrp		Senior of Water, associated with Luna.
Laoazrp	AC:C	
lap	lap	for (conj.)
lape	AC:C, G, VV	
Laparin		Governor of the Second Division of the Aethyr *Zim.*
larag	la-raj	nor.
laraji	AC:C	
larasada	AC:C, G	=*lrasd,* dispose.

larianu*	AC:G	=*trian,* shall be.
larinuji	AC:C, G	=*lring,* stir up.
Larz		angel, companion of *Rlza.*
las **lasa**	las AC:C	rich.
Lasben		angel who appeared to Dee and Kelley.
lasdi **lusdi**	laz-di GD	foot, feet. Also *lusd.*
lava		pray.
Lavacon **Lanacon**	 AC:C	Governor of the Second Division of the Aethyr *Lea.*
Lavavoth		angelic King ruling in the South-South-West.
Lazdixi		Governor of the First Division of the Aethyr *Lit.*
Lea		name of the Sixteenth Aethyr.
Leaoc		angel also known as *Leoc.*
lehusan		(meaning unknown).
lehuslach		(meaning unknown).
lel	lel	same. Cf. *l.*
Leoc		angel skilled in finding metals and precious stones, ruled by *Nelapr Omebb.* Also *Leaoc.*
lephe		(meaning unknown).
Levanael **Leveanael**		planetary angel, associated with Luna.
levithmong **leuitahemonuji**	le-vith-mong AC:C	beast (of the field), cattle.

Lexarph		Governor of the First Division of the Aethyr *Zax*.
Lgaiol		=*Slgaiol,* Senior of Water.
Lhctga		=*Alhctga,* Senior of Earth.
Lhiansa **Liiansa**	 AC:C	Senior of Earth, associated with Saturn.
li		first. Cf. *l, la, lo.*
liaida*	AC:G	=*laiad,* secret.
Liba		angel (Filius Filiorum Lucis), associated with Jupiter.
li-el	AC:C	=*l,* first.
Ligdisa		Senior of Water, associated with Saturn.
Liiansa	AC:C	=*Lhiansa,* Senior of Earth.
Lil		name of the First Aethyr.
lilonon **iisononu*** **ilonon**	li-lo-non AC:C GD	branch, branches.
limlal	lim-lal	treasure.
Lin		name of the Twenty-Second Aethyr.
Lit		name of the Fifth Aethyr.
Lixipsp	AC:VV	warden of the Aethyr *Bag.*
Llacza **Ilacza** **Olacza**		Divine Name of Six Letters, ruling Water of Air.
Llpiz		Divine Name of Five Letters, ruling Fire of Earth.
Lmag **Lmmag**		angel, companion of *Magl.*

loadohi	lo-a-do-hi	kingdom. Also *londoh.*
adohi*	GD	
adoho*	AC:C	
loangab		(meaning unknown).
Loe		name of the Twelfth Aethyr.
loagaeth		speech from God. The name of a book by the angels, *Liber Logaeth.*
logaeth		
logaah		
logah		
loholo	lo-ho-lo	shine.
sobolo	AC:C, GD	
lolcis	lol-sis	buckler.
lolacis	AC:C	
loncho	lon-cho	fall.
lonucaho	AC:C	
lonukaho	AC:G	
londoh	lon-do	kingdom. Also *loadohi.*
londohe	AC:C	
lonudohe	AC:C	
lonsa	lon-sa	power. Also *lansh.*
lonshi	lon-shi	
lonshin	lon-shin	
lonsh	GD	
lonu-sahi-toxa	AC:C	= *lonshi tox,* power of her.
lorslq	lor-sel-kwa	flower, flowers.
lores-el-qo	AC:C	
lrasd	el-razd	dispose.
larasada	AC:C, G	
lring	el-ring	stir up.
larinuji	AC:C, G	
Lrxn		angel, companion of *Nlrx.*
Lrixn		

Lsrahpm		Senior of Water, associated with Mars.
lu	lu	nor.
Luah **Luach**		praising angels.
lucal **lucala**	lu-kal AC:C, G	north.
luciftian **luciftias** **lucifatianu** **lukiftias**	lu-sif-ti-an lu-sif-ti-as AC:C AC:C	brightness.
luiahe	lu-ya-he	song.
lulo		tartar (or mother of vinegar).
lurfando		(meaning unknown).
lusd **lusda** **lusdan** **lusdi**	luzd luz-da luz-dan GD	foot, feet. Also *lasdi.*
luseroth		(meaning unknown).

M Tal

m	em	1) nine. Also *em*. 2) except (GD *in*).
maasi	mā-si	laid up.
mabberam		(meaning unknown).
mabza	mab-za	coat.
mabezoda	AC:C	
Mad	mad	God. Cf. *Iad, Oiad, Piad.*
mada	AC:C, G	
madariatza	AC:C	= *madriax,* heaven.
madarida	AC:C, G	= *madrid,* iniquity.
madariitza	AC:G	= *madriax,* heaven.
madariiatza	AC:C	
Madimi		angel (Filia Filiarum Lucis), associated with Mercury.
Madimiel		planetary angel presiding over the sphere of Mars.
madriax	mad-ri-ax	heaven. Cf. *oadriax.*
madriiax	mad-ri-ax	
madriaax	GD	
madariatza	AC:C	
madariitza	AC:G	
madariiatza	AC:C	
madrid	mad-rid	iniquity, iniquities.
madarida	AC:C	
maelpereji	AC:C, G	= *malprg,* fire.
Magl		angel powerful in mechanical aids, ruled by the angel *Pmagl* and *Maladi Olaad.* Also

		Mamgl. Companions are *Aglm, Glma, Lmag.*
Magm		angel skilled in finding metals and precious stones, ruled by *Nelapr Omebb.* Also *Masgm.*
mahorela	AC: VV	dark heavens. Cf. *madriax.*
Maladi		Divine Name of Six Letters, ruling Earth of Water.
Malap		demonic name (reversal of *Palam*) commanding cacodemons of Water of Air.
malprg	mal-përj	fire, fires; fiery darts.
malpirgi	mal-përji	
maelpereji	AC: C, G	
malapereji	AC: C	
malapireji	AC: C	
Mals		name of the Enochian letter representing P.
Mamgl		angel also known as *Magl.*
manada*	AC: C	see *smnad,* another.
manin	ma-nin	mind (n.).
maninu	AC: C	
maoffas	ma-of-fas	measure, be measured.
maof-fasa	AC: C	
MAPM		9639.
meapeme	AC: C	
Mapsama		angel who appeared to Dee and Kelley; the name means 'Tell them'.
marb	marb	according to.
marebe	AC: C, G	
marebi	AC: G	
mariehe*	AC: G	

Masgm		angel also known as *Magm.*
Matb		thousand
matabe	AC:C	
Mathula		Governor of the Second Division of the Aethyr *Zaa.*
Mathvla	AC:C	
matorb	ma-torb	echoing.
mtorebe	AC:C	
Maz		name of the Sixth Aethyr.
Me		angel (Filia Lucis), associated with Luna.
Med		name of the Enochian letter representing O.
Meeana		demonic name (reversal of *Anaeem*) commanding cacodemons of Water of Earth.
Merifri		=*Murifri,* angel.
Mfzrn		demonic name (reversal of *Nrzfm*) commanding cacodemons of Fire of Fire.
Mgm		cacodemon, counterpart of the angel *Gmnm.*
miam	mi-am	continuance. Cf. *nuam.*
mian	mi-an	
miame	AC:C	
MIAN		3663.
mianu	AC:C	
Miao		angel, companion of *Iaom.* Also *Misao.*
micalp	mi-kalp	mightier. Cf. *cruscanse.*
micalapape	AC:C	

micalz	mi-kalz	power; powerful, mighty.
micalzo	mi-kal-zo	Cf. *canse, drilpa, lonsa.*
micaolz	mi-kalz	
micaelazodo	AC:G	
micaelzodo	AC:G	
micalazoda	AC:C	
micalazodo	AC:C	
micaolazoda	AC:C	
mikaelzodo	AC:G	
micma	mik-ma	behold.
micama	AC:C, G	
miinoag	mī-nōj	corner.
miinoagi	AC:C	
miketh		wisdom (?)
mir	mir	torment (n.)
mire	AC:G	
mirc	mirk	upon.
mireca	AC:C	
mireka	AC:C	
Mirzind		Governor of the First Division of the Aethyr *Uti.*
Misao		angel also known as *Miao.*
Miz		cacodemon, counterpart of the angel *Izxp.*
Mma		cacodemon, counterpart of the angel *Magm.*
moanu*	AC:C	=*ooanoan,* eyes.
Moc		cacodemon, counterpart of the angel *Ocnm.*
molap	mo-lap	man, men.
Molpand		Governor of the First Division of the Aethyr *Ich.*

molvi **molui**	mol-vi AC:C	surge.
mom	mom	moss.
momao	mo-mau	crown (n.) Cf. *momar.*
momar **momare**	mo-mar AC:C	crown (v.), be crowned.
monasci **monasaci**	mo-nas-ki AC:C	name. Cf. *omaoas.*
monons **mononusa**	mo-nonz AC:C	heart.
moooah **moooabe***	mō-wa AC:C	repent, regret.
Mop		cacodemon, counterpart of the angel *Opmn.*
Mor		Holy Name of Three Letters, ruling the Element of Earth.
Moreorgran **Morvorgran**		angel who appeared to Dee and Kelley.
mospleh **mos-pelehe**	mos-ple AC:C	horn.
Mot		cacodemon, counterpart of the angel *Otoi.*
moz		joy.
mozod		joy of God.
Mph		Holy Name of Three Letters, ruling the Element of Water.
Mrx		cacodemon, counterpart of the angel *Rxnl.*
Msal **Msmal**		angel ruled by *Spmnir Llpiz.*

Mtdi **Mtndi**		angel, companion of *Tdim.*
Mto		cacodemon, counterpart of the angel *Toco.*
mtorebe	AC:C	= *matorb,* echoing.
Murifri **Merifri**		angel who appeared to Dee and Kelley on 2 June 1583.

N Drux

Na		Lord of Hosts; Trinity. Cf. *Enay.*
na **na-hath**	GD	name of the Enochian letter representing H.
na	AC:VV	that.
Naaa		angel, companion of *Anaa.* Also *Navaa.*
Nabaomi		Governor of the First Division of the Aethyr *Zen.*
na-e-el	AC:G	=*nanaeel,* power.
na-hath	GD	=*na,* Enochian letter.
nai		(meaning unknown).
Nalvage		angel who appeared to Dee and Kelley on 11 February 1584; his name means 'Avoidance of earthly things' *(fuga terrestrium).* Nalvage, a near kinsman of Madimi's mother, was the principal dictator of the Enochian Calls.
nanaeel	na-nai-el	power. Cf. *micalz, lonsa.*
nanba **nanuba**	nan-ba AC:C	thorn, thorns.
Nanta		spirit of Earth.
Naoo **Naooo**		angel powerful in transformation, ruled by *Aiaoai Oiiit.*
napta **napeai**	nap-ta na-pe-ai	sword, swords. Also *nazpsad.*

napea	GD	
napeta	AC:C	
Navaa		angel also known as *Naaa.*
nax		(meaning unknown).
naz	naz	pillar, pillars. Cf. *nazarth, nazavabh.*
nazoda	AC:C, G	
nazarth	naz-arth	pillars of gladness. Cf. *naz.*
na-zodaretahe	AC:C	
nazavabh	naz-a-vab	hyacinth pillars. Cf. *naz.*
na-zodavabebe*	AC:C	
nazpsad	naz-psad	sword, swords. Also *napta.*
nazps	GD	
nazodapesad	AC:C, G	
Nbrc		angel, companion of *Cnbr.*
Nbarc		
Ndazn		angel also known as *Ndzn.*
Ndnos		demonic name (reversal of *Sondn*) commanding cacodemons of Water of Earth.
ne		holy.
Ndzn		angel powerful in transformation, ruled by *Maladi Olaad.* Also *Ndazn.*
Nelapr		Divine Name of Six Letters, ruling Water of Water.
nenni	AC:VV	you have become. Cf. *noan.*
neph		(meaning unknown).
netaab	ne-tab	government, governing.
netaaib	ne-taib	
netab	ne-tab	

netaabe	AC:C	
netaaibe	AC:C	
Nhdd		angel skilled in medicine,
Nhodd		ruled by *Obgota Aabco.*
NI		28.
Nia		name of the Twenty-Fourth Aethyr.
nibm	nib-ëm	season. Cf. *capimao.*
nidali	ni-da-li	noise, noises.
Nigrana		Governor of the Second Division of the Aethyr *Des.*
niis	nīs	come, come away, come forth.
niisa	nī-sa	
niiso	nī-so	
ninu	AC:C	see *ulcinin,* happy.
Nlrx		angel powerful in finding out
Nlirx		secrets of men, ruled by the angel *Pnlrx* and *Iaaasd Atapa.* Companions are *Lrxn, Rxnl, Xnlr.*
Noalmr		Divine Name of Six Letters, ruling Air of Fire.
noan	no-an	be, become.
noaln	no-aln	
noar	no-ar	
noas	no-as	
noasmi	no-as-mi	
noanu	AC:C	
noalanu	AC:C	
noari	AC:C	
noasa	AC:C	
noasami	AC:C	

Word	Pronunciation	Meaning
nobloh	nob-lo	palm, palms (of hand).
nobeloha	AC:C	
Nocamal		Governor of the Second Division of the Aethyr *Lit*.
Nociabi		Governor of the Second Division of the Aethyr *Oxo*.
noco	no-ko	servant. Cf. *booapis*.
nofahon*	AC:G	=*nothoa,* midst.
Nogahel		planetary angel presiding over the sphere of Venus.
noib	noib	yea.
noibe	AC:C	
nomig	no-mij	even as.
nomiji	AC:C, G	
nonca	non-sa	you, to you. Cf. *vomsarg, g*.
noncf	nonsf	
nonci	non-si	
noncp	nonsp	
nonuca	AC:C	
nonucafe	AC:C	
nonuci	AC:C	
nonucape	AC:C	
nonuji*	AC:G	
noqod	nok-wod	servant, minister. Cf. *noco, booapis*.
noquodi	nok-wo-di	
noquol	nok-wol	
noqodi	AC:C	
noquod	GD	
nor	nor	son, sons. Also *noromi*.
nore	AC:G	
norezoda	AC:G	=*norz,* six.
norezodacahisa	AC:C	=*norz chis,* six are.

noromi	no-ro-mi	son, sons. Also *nor.*
noroni*	AC:C	
norz	norz	six.
norezoda	AC:G	
nostoah		it was (?)
nothoa	no-thoa	midst; among, amidst.
notahoa	AC:C, G	
nofahon*	AC:G	
Npat		angel ruled by *Aourrz Aloai.*
Nprat		
Nroa		angel, companion of *Roan.*
Nrcoa		
Nrzfm		Divine Name of Five Letters, ruling Fire of Fire.
nuam	nu-am	continuance. Cf. *miam.*
nuame	AC:C	

O Med

o	o	five.
Oacnr		angel, also known as *Oanr*.
oadariatza	AC:C	=*oadriax*, lower heavens.
oado	o-a-do	weave.
oadriax	o-ad-ri-ax	lower heavens. Cf. *madriax*.
oadariatza	AC:C	
oai	o-ai	amongst. Also *aaf*, *aai*, *aao*, *eai*.
Oalco		=*Aabco*, Divine Name.
oali	o-a-li	place, put. Cf. *aala*.
oeli	AC:C	
oanio	o-a-ni-o	moment.
Oanr		angel, companion of *Roan*. Also *Oacnr*.
Oap		cacodemon, counterpart of the angel *Apst*.
OB		28.
Obava		Divine Name of Five Letters, ruling Water of Fire.
Obelison		a title of the angelic Prince *Befafes:* 'Pleasant Deliverer'. Cf. *obelisong*.
obelisong	o-be-li-song	deliverer. Cf. *zonrensg*.
obelisonugi	AC:C, G	
obelisonuji	AC:G	
obeloce	AC:C	=*obloc*, garland.
obezoda	AC:C	=*obza*, half.

obloc	ob-lok	garland.
obeloce	AC:C	
Obgota		Divine Name of Six Letters, ruling Air of Water.
Olgota		
Oblgota	GD	
Obmacas		Governor of the First Division of the Aethyr *Deo.*
oboleh	o-bo-le	garment.
obolehe	AC:C	
Obvaors		Governor of the Second Division of the Aethyr *Uti.*
Obuaors	AC:C	
obza	ob-za	half.
obezoda	AC:C	
Ocanm		angel, also known as *Ocnm.*
Ocbaa		demonic name (reversal of *Aabco*) commanding cacodemons of Air of Water.
Occodon		Governor of the First Division of the Aethyr *Lil.*
Ocnm		angel powerful in transformation, ruled by *Cbalpt Arbiz.*
od	od	and.
odazodi	AC:C	see *acroodzi,* beginning.
Oddiorg		Governor of the First Division of the Aethyr *Zip.*
odo	o-do	1) open. 2) cacodemon, counterpart of the angel *Doop.*
Odraxti		Governor of the Second Division of the Aethyr *Rii.*

Odxlov		demonic name (reversal of *Volxdo*) commanding cacodemons of Earth of Fire.
Oec		cacodemon, counterpart of the angel *Ecop*.
oecrimi	o-ek-ri-mi	praise (v.), sing praises.
oe-cari-mi	AC:C	Cf. *ecrin, rest*.
oekarimi	AC:G	
iecarimi*	AC:C	
oela	AC:G	=*ol,* make.
oeli	AC:C	=*oali,* place.
ofafafe	o-fa-fa-fe	vial. Also *efafafe*.
ofekufa	AC:VV	elevated, lifted up.
Ogiodi		demonic name (reversal of *Idoigo*) commanding cacodemons of Air of Air.
oheloka	AC:G	duke.
ohio	o-hi-o	woe.
ohyo	AC:C	
oholera*	AC:G	=*ohorela,* make law.
Ohooohaatan		Great Elemental King of Fire.
ohorela	o-ho-re-la	make a law, legislate.
oholera*	AC:G	
oi	oi	this.
Oia		cacodemon, counterpart of the angel *Iaba*.
Oiad	o-yad	God, the Just One. Cf. *Iad,*
Oiada	AC:C, G	*Mad*.
Oiiit		Divine Name of Five Letters, ruling Earth of Air.

Oip		Holy Name of Three Letters, ruling the Element of Fire.
o-isalamahe*	AC:C	= *oi salman,* this house.
okada	AC:G	mercy.
ol **ole**	ol AC:C	1) I, myself. 2) make. Cf. *eol, oln.* 3) 24; one twenty-fourth.
Olaad		Divine Name of Five Letters, ruling Earth of Water.
Olacza		= *Llacza,* Divine Name.
olaho	AC:VV	for the second time. Cf. *olani.*
olalogi	AC:C	= *ollog,* man.
olalore	AC:C, G	= *ollor,* man.
olani	o-la-ni	twice.
olanu	AC:C	= *oln,* made.
olapireta	AC:C, G	= *olpirt,* light.
ole	AC:C	= *ol,* one twenty-fourth.
Olgota		= *Obgota,* Divine Name.
ollog **ollor** **olalogi** **olalore**	ol-og ol-or AC:C AC:C, G	man, men. Cf. *morlap, olora.*
oln **olanu**	oln AC:C	made. Cf. *ol, eol.*
Oloag		Divine Name of Five Letters, ruling Air of Fire.
olora	ol-o-ra	(of) man. Cf. *ollag, morlap.*
Olpaged		angelic King ruling in the East.

Word	Pronunciation / Source	Meaning
olpirt	ol-përt	light.
olprt	GD	
olapireta	AC:C, G	
om	om	1) understand, know. Also *omax*. Cf. *oma, ixomaxip*. 2) we, us.
ome	AC:C	
oma	o-ma	understanding. Cf. *om*.
omp	omp	
omepe	AC:G	
Omagg		angel, also known as *Omgg*.
Omagrap		Governor of the Third Division of the Aethyr *Pop*.
omaoas	o-ma-was	name. Cf. *dooain, monasci*.
omaoasa	AC:C, G	
omaosa	AC:G	
omax	om-ax	know. Also *om*. Cf. *oma, ixomaxip*.
omaxa	AC:C	
ome	AC:C	= *om, know*.
Omebb		Divine Name of Five Letters, ruling Water of Water.
omepe	AC:C	= *omp*, understanding.
ome-petilabe	AC:C	= *omp tilb*, her understanding.
Omgg		angel skilled in finding metals and precious stones, ruled by *Anaeem Sondn*. Also *Omagg*.
Omia		angel, companion of *Iaom*. Also *Omsia*.
omicaolz	o-mi-kalz	be mighty. Cf. *micalz*.
omp		= *oma*, understanding.
Omsia		angel, also known as *Omia*.
omsomna		(meaning unknown).

on	AC:VV	made, built. Cf. *oln.*
Ona		cacodemon, counterpart of the angel *Naoo.*
ondoh*	GD	= *londoh,* kingdom.
Onh		cacodemon, counterpart of the angel *Nhdd.*
Onizimp		Governor of the Second Division of the Aethyr *Tor.*
Onp		cacodemon, counterpart of the angel *Npat.*
ooa* **ooain***	AC:C GD	See *ooanoan,* eye.
Ooanamb		Governor of the Third Division of the Aethyr *Uta.*
ooanoan **ooaona** **ooa*** **ooain***	ō-a-no-an ō-a-o-na AC:C GD	eye, eyes.
ooge	ō-ge	chamber.
Oopz **Oodpz**		angel powerful in transformation, ruled by *Volxdo Sioda.*
OP **ope**	 AC:C	22.
Opad		angel, companion of *Dopa.* Also *Opnad.*
Opmn **Opamn**		angel skilled in medicine, ruled by *Noalmr Oloag.*
Opna **Opana**		angel powerful in transformation, ruled by *Cbalpt Arbiz.*

Opnad		angel, also known as *Opad.*
oq **o-quo**	ok AC:C	but. Cf. *crip.*
or **orth**	 GD	name of the Enochian letter representing F.
Orcanin **Orcamir**	 AC:C	Governor of the First Division of the Aethyr *Nia.*
oreri	AC:C, G	=*orri,* stone.
oresa	AC:C, G	=*ors,* darkness.
oresaba	AC:C	=*orsba,* drunken.
oresacore	AC:C	=*orscor,* dryness.
oresaha*	AC:C	=*orsba,* drunken.
Orh		name of a spirit. ('The word has 72 significations').
Ormn		angel skilled in medicine, ruled by *Angpoi Unnax.* Also *Orpmn.*
Oro		Holy Name of Three Letters, ruling the Element of Air.
oroch **orocha** **orocahe** **orocaha**	o-roch o-ro-cha AC:C AC:C	under, underneath.
Orpanib **Orpamb**	 AC:C	Governor of the Third Division of the Aethyr *Zaa.*
Orpmn		angel, also known as *Ormn.*
orri **oreri**	or-ri AC:C, G	stone. Cf. *patralx.*
ors **oresa**	orz AC:C, G	darkness.

orsba	orz-ba	drunken.
oresaba	AC:C	
orsca	orz-ka	building, buildings.
orscor	orz-kor	dryness.
oresacore	AC:C	
orth	GD	= *or*, Enochian letter representing F.
os	os	twelve.
osf	osf	discord.
othil	o-thil	1) set; I have set.
otahil	AC:C	2) seat, seats. Cf. *thil.*
otahila	AC:C, G	
Otoi		angel ruled by *Aourrz Aloai.*
Otroi		
oucho	u-cho	confound.
ovcho	GD	
oucaho	AC:G	
ovankaho*	AC:G	
ovoars	o-vo-arz	centre.
ouoaresa	AC:G	
ovof	ov-of	magnify, be magnified.
OX		26.
oxex	ox-ex	vomit.
oxiayal	ox-i-ai-al	mighty seat, throne.
Oxlopar		Governor of the Third Division of the Aethyr *Bag.*
Oxo		name of the Fifteenth Aethyr.
oxox		(meaning unknown).
Oyub		angel skilled in finding metals and precious stones, ruled by *Llacza Palam.*
Oyaub		

Ozab		angel, companion of *Boza.*
Ozaab		
ozazm	o zaz-ëm	make (me), make (us). Cf. *ol.*
ozazma	o-zaz-ma	
ozozma	GD	
ozadazodame	AC:C	
ozodazodama	AC:C	
Ozidaia		Governor of the First Division of the Aethyr *Lin.*
ozien	o-zin	hand. Cf. *zien.*
ozol	o-zol	
ozodien	AC:C	
ozodola	AC:C	
ozongon	o-zong-on	wind, winds. Also *zong.*
ozodonugonu	AC:C	

P Mals

p	pi	eight.
pa **pe**	GD	name of the Enochian letter representing B.
paaox	pa-ox	remain.
paaoxt	pa-oxt	
pa-aolza*	AC:G	
pa-aotza	AC:G	
paaotzata	AC:C	
pa-iotz	AC:G	
pa-iotza	AC:G	
pacaduasam		(meaning unknown).
pacaph		(meaning unknown).
Pacasna		Governor of the Second Division of the Aethyr *Arn.*
Paco		angel powerful in transformation, ruled by *Maladi Olaad.* Also *Palco.*
padgze		justice from the Divine Power, without blemish.
Pado		angel, companion of *Dopa.* Also *Pando.*
paeb	paib	oak.
paebe	AC:C	
Paeoc		angel, also known as *Paoc.*
page	pa-ge	rest.
paje	AC:C	
paid	paid	always.
paida	AC:C, G	

pa-iotz	AC:G	=*paaox,* remain.
pa-iotza	AC:G	
pajeipe	AC:C	=*page ip,* rest not.
pajo-ooaoanu	AC:G	=*pugo ooaona,* to eyes.
pal	GD	name of the Enochian letter representing X.
pala		two (separated), pair. Cf. *pola.*
Palam		Divine Name of Five Letters, ruling Water of Air.
Palco		angel, also known as *Paco.*
Pali		angel ruled by *Rzionr Nrzfm.* Also *Panli.*
Palut		angel, also known as *Paut.*
pambt	pamt	unto (me).
pamebeta	AC:C	
pamphicas		(meaning unknown: a contemptuous word).
Pando		angel, also known as *Pado.*
Panli		angel, also known as *Pali.*
panpir	pan-për	pour (down).
panupire	AC:C	
Paoc		angel skilled in finding metals and precious stones, ruled by *Llacza Palam.* Also *Paeoc.*
paombd	pāmd	member, members.
paomebeda	AC:C	
papnor	pap-nor	remembrance, memory.
papenore	AC:C	
par	par	they, them; in them.
pare	AC:C	

parach	par-ak	equal.
paracahe	AC:C	
paracleda	pa-ra-kle-da	wedding.
paracaleda	AC:C	
paradial	pa-ra-di-al	dwelling, dwellings; living
pa-ra-diala	AC:C	dwellings.
paradiz	pa-ra-diz	virgin.
paradizod	AC:C	
para-di-zoda	AC:C	
Paraoan		Governor of the Second Division of the Aethyr *Lin.*
pare	AC:C	=*par,* they.
pare-meji	AC:C	=*parm gi,* run with.
parm	parm	run.
pareme	AC:C	
Parziba		Governor of the Second Division of the Aethyr *Chr.*
pasbs	pazbz	daughter, daughters.
pashs	GD	
pasahasa	AC:C	
Pascomb		Governor of the Second
Paxcomb		Division of the Aethyr *Lil.*
patralx	pat-ralx	rock (n.) Cf. *orri.*
pataralaxa	AC:C	
Paulacarp		name of an evil spirit.
Paut		angel, companion of *Utpa.* Also *Palut.*
Paxcomb		=*Pascomb,* Governor.
Paz		name of the Fourth Aethyr.
PD		33.
peda	AC:C	

Pdi		cacodemon, counterpart of the angel *Diri.*
Pdoce		Holy Name of Five Letters, ruling the Element of Fire.
Pedoce	GD	
pe	GD	=*pa,* Enochian letter representing B.
pe-iad	AC:C	=*Piad,* God.
pelapeli	AC:C	=*plapli,* partaker.
peleh		(meaning unknown).
pelosi	AC:C	=*plosi,* many.
PEOAL		69636.
peranuta	AC:G	see *adrpan,* cast down.
peredazodare	AC:C	=*prdzar,* diminish.
peregi	AC:G	=*prge, prgel,* fire.
pereje	AC:C, G	
pereji	AC:G	
perejela	AC:C	
pereta	AC:C	see *ialprt,* flame.
periazoda	AC:C	=*priaz, priazi,* those.
periazodi	AC:C	
perifa*	AC:C	=*praf,* dwell.
peripsax	pe-rip-sax	heaven. Cf. *madriax.*
peripsol	pe-rip-sol	
piripsol	pi-rip-sol	
piripson	pi-rip-son	
pi-ripesonu	AC:C	
peripesatza	AC:C	
peripesol	AC:C, G	
piripsax	GD	
Pfm		cacodemon, counterpart of the angel *Fmna.*

phama		I will give.
Phanael		angel who appeared to Dee and Kelley.
Phra **Phara**		angel powerful in change of place, ruled by the angel *Ephra* and *Anaeem Sondn.* Companions are *Hrap, Raph, Aphr.*
pi	pi	1) place (n.) 2) she.
Pia		cacodemon, counterpart of the angel *Iahl.*
Piad	pi-ad	God. Cf. *Iad, Mad, Oiad.*
piadph **pi-adapahe** **pi-adapehe** **pi-adph**	pi-adf AC:G AC:C, G GD	jaw, jaws.
piamol **piamoel**	pi-a-mol AC:C, GD	righteousness.
pian **pianu**	GD AC:C	See *aspian,* quality.
piap **piape**	pi-ap AC:C, G; GD	balance (n.)
pi-beliare	AC:C	=*pi bliar,* places of comfort.
pidiai	pi-di-ai	sleeve, marble sleeves.
pii	GD	=*pi i,* she is.
pilada	AC:C	=*pild,* continually.
pilah **pilahe**	pi-la AC:C, G	moreover.
pild **pilada**	pild AC:C	continually.

pilzin	pil-zin	firmament of waters.
pil-zodinu	AC:C	
pinzu-a		(meaning unknown).
Pir	pīr	Holy One, Holy Ones.
Pire	AC:C, G	
pire	AC:VV	holy.
pireda	AC:VV	
pi-ripesonu	AC:C	=*peripsax,* heaven.
piripsax	GD	
piripsol		
piripson		
Piz		cacodemon, counterpart of the angel *Iznr.*
pizi	GD	See *amipzi,* fasten.
plapli	plap-li	partaker, partakers.
pelapeli	AC:C	
plosi	plo-zi	many, as many.
pelosi	AC:C	
Pmagl		angel ruling *Magl* and companions.
Pmox		angel ruled by *Aourzz Aloai.*
Pmzox		
poamal	po-a-mal	palace.
poamalzod	po-a-mal-zod	
poamala	AC:C	
pooumala	AC:G	
proamal*	AC:G	
Pocisini	AC:VV	=*Focisni,* Governor.
poilp	poilp	divide. Cf. *yrpoil.*
poilape	AC:C, G	
pola		two (together), *pair.* Cf. *pala.*

Ponodol		Governor of the Third Division of the Aethyr *Ich.*
pooumala	AC:G	=*poamal,* palace.
Pop		name of the Nineteenth Aethyr.
Pophand		Governor of the First Division of the Aethyr *Des.*
Pothnir		Governor of the Third Division of the Aethyr *Paz.*
Ppsac		angel ruling *Psac* and companions.
praf	praf	dwell (in). Cf. *faonts, pragma.*
perifa*	AC:C	
pragma		dwell(?) Cf. *praf, faonts.*
prdzar	për-dzar	diminish.
peredazodare	AC:C	
prge	përj	fire.
prgel	për-jel	
peregi	AC:G	
pereje	AC:C, G	
pereji	AC:G	
perejela	AC:C	
priaz	pri-az	those.
priazi	pri-a-zi	
periazoda	AC:C	
periazodi	AC:C	
Pristac		Governor of the Third Division of the Aethyr *Zid.*
proamal*	AC:G	=*poamal,* palace.
Psac		angel powerful in mechanical arts, ruled by the angel *Ppsac*
Psuac		

		and *Volxdo Sioda.* Companions are *Sacp, Acps, Cpsa.*
pugo	pu-go	unto.
pujo	AC:G	
puje	AC:G	
puim	pu-im	sickle, sickles.
puin*		
pu-ime	AC:C, G	
puje	AC:G	=*pugo,* unto.
pujo	AC:G	
Pxinbal	AC:VV	=*Labnixp,* Governor.
Pziza		angel ruling *Ziza* and companions.

Q Ger

q	kwa	or.
qo	AC:C	
q	kwa	1) thy.
quo	AC:C	2) content, contents.
qaa	kwā	garment, garments.
qaa	kwā	creation. Cf. *qaal.*
qaan	kwān	
qaaon	kwān	
qaas	kwās	
quaa	AC:G	
qa-a-an	GD	
qo-a-an	AC:C	
qaa-om	GD	
qoaanu	AC:G	
qua-a-on	AC:G	
go-a-anu*	AC:G	
qaal	kwāl	creator. Cf. *qaa.*
qadah	kwā-dā	
qo-a-al	AC:G	
qo-o-al	AC:G	
qo-o-ala	AC:G	
quo-o-al	AC:G	
go-o-al*	AC:G	
qaada	GD	
quo-a-dahe	AC:C	
qanis	GD	=*quanis,* olive.
qouodi	AC:G	see *noquod,* minister.
qting	kwë-ting	rotten.
qotinuji	AC:C	
quanis	kwa-nis	olive, olives.
qanis	GD	

QUAR		1636.
quare	AC:C	
quasahi	kwa-sa-hi	pleasure
quasb	kwazb	destroy.
quasaba	AC:G	
quasabe	AC:C, G	
quasahe*	AC:G	
quiin	kwīn	wherein.
quiinu	AC:C, G	
quo-a-al	AC:C, G	= *qaal,* creator.
quo-a-asa	AC:C	= *qaas,* creation.
quo-a-dahe	AC:C	= *qadah,* creator.
quo-o-al	AC:G	= *qaal,* creator.
quo-o-i-ape	AC:G	by the name. Cf. *dooiap.*
qurlst	kwërlst	handmaid.
qurelesata	AC:C	

R Don

Raagios		Elemental King of Water, associated with Sol.
Raagiol		
Raagiosl		
Raagiosel	AC:C	
Raaph		angel, also known as *Raph.*
raas	rās	east.
raasy	rā-sy	
ra-asa	AC:C	
raasyo	AC:C	
raclir	rak-lir	weeping.
racalire	AC:C	
Rad		cacodemon, counterpart of the angel *Adre.*
Ranglam		Governor of the Third Division of the Aethyr *Uti.*
Raph		angel, companion of *Phra.*
Rapolxo	AC:VV	= *Oxlopar,* Governor.
Rbnh		angel skilled in finding metals and precious stones, ruled by *Llacza Palam.*
Rbznh		
Rcnb		angel, companion of *Cnbr.*
Rcanb		
Rda		cacodemon, counterpart of the angel *Datt.*
resat-el	AC:C	= *rest el,* praise Him.
rest	rest	praise (v.) Cf. *oecrimi.*
Rgan		angel powerful in transformation, ruled by *Volxdo Sioda.*
Rgoan		

Rii		name of the Twenty-Ninth Aethyr.
Rinmps		demonic name (reversal of *Spmnir*) commanding cacodemons of Fire of Earth.
rior **riore**	ri-or AC:C	widow.
ripir **ripire**	ri-pir AC:C	no place. Cf. *pi*.
rit **rita**	rit AC:C	mercy. Cf. *iehusoz*.
Rlmu **Rlemu**		angel skilled in finding metals and precious stones, ruled by *Anaeem Sondn*.
rlodnr		furnace (?), crucible (?)
Rmlaon		demonic name (reversal of *Noalmr*) commanding cacodemons of Air of Fire.
Rnoizr		demonic name (reversal of *Rzionr*) commanding cacodemons of Fire of Earth.
Roan **Rocan**		angel powerful in mechanical arts, ruled by the angel *Hroan* and *Cbalpt Arbiz*. Companions are *Oanr, Anro, Nroa*.
Rocle **Iocle**	 AC:C	angel (Filius Filiorum Lucis) associated with Mars.
Ronoamb		Governor of the First Division of the Aethyr *Tor*.
ror **roray** **rore**	ror AC:C, G AC:G	sun.

rowgh		(meaning unknown).
roxtan		wine.
Rpa		cacodemon, counterpart of the angel *Paco.*
Rpalen		demonic name (reversal of *Nelapr*) commanding cacodemons of Water of Water.
Rrb		cacodemon, counterpart of the angel *Rbnh.*
Rrl		cacodemon, counterpart of the angel *Rlmu.*
rsam	rë-sam	admiration.
Rsi		cacodemon, counterpart of the angel *Sias.*
Rsni **Rsoni**		angel skilled in medicine, ruled by *Angpoi Unnax.*
rudna		(meaning unknown).
Ruoi **Ruroi**		angel skilled in finding metals and precious stones, ruled by *Nelapr Omebb.*
Rxao		angel powerful in transformation, ruled by *Cbalpt Arbiz.* Also *Rxpao.*
Rxnl **Rxinl**		angel, companion of *Nrlx.*
Rxp		cacodemon, counterpart of the angel *Xpcn.*
Rxpao		angel, also known as *Rxao.*
Rzionr		Divine Name of Six Letters, ruling Fire of Fire.

Rzla
Rzila

angel powerful in mixtures of natures, ruled by the angel *Erzla* and *Idoigo Ardza*. Companions are *Zlar, Larz, Arzl*.

S Fam

S		1) four, fourth. 2) angel (Filia Filiarum Lucis) associated with Sol.
sa	AC:G	and.
sa	GD	see *saga,* entire.
Saaiz		angel, also known as *Saiz.*
saanir **saanire**	sā-nir AC:C	part, parts.
saba		= *soba,* whose.
Sabathiel		planetary angel presiding over the sphere of Saturn.
Sach		confirming angels.
Sacp		angel, companion of *Psac.* Also *Saucp.*
sa-div	AC:C	= *s diu,* fourth angle.
saga	sa-ga	one, entire, whole.
Saiinou **Saiinov**	 AC:C	Senior of Water, associated with Jupiter.
Saiz		angel skilled in medicine, ruled by *Obgota Aabco.* Also *Saaiz.*
salabaiotza* **salabarotza** **salaberoxa** **salaberotza**	AC:G AC:G AC:C AC:G	= *salbrox,* sulphur.
salada	AC:C, G	= *sald,* wonder.
salamanu **salamann***	AC:C, G AC:G	= *salman,* house.

salbrox	sal-brox	sulphur. Cf. *dlasod.*
salabaiotza*	AC:G	
salabarotza	AC:G	
salaberoxa	AC:C	
salaberotza	AC:G	
sald	sald	wonder, wonders (n.) Cf. *zirn.*
salada	AC:C, G	
ald*	GD	
salman	sal-man	house.
salamanu	AC:C, G	
salamann*	AC:G	
Samapha		Governor of the First Division of the Aethyr *Zom.*
same*	AC:C	= *om,* know.
samvelg	sam-velj	righteous. Cf. *balit.*
samevelaji	AC:C	
sapah	sa-pa	sound, sounds; mighty sounds.
sapahe	AC:C, G	
Saucp		angel, also known as *Sacp.*
Saxtomp		Governor of the First Division of the Aethyr *Maz.*
sayomepe	AC:C	= *symp,* another.
Saziami		Governor of the First Division of the Aethyr *Zaa.*
Scio		angel skilled in medicine, ruled by *Noalmr Oloag.*
Scmio		
sembabam		(meaning unknown).
Semeliel		planetary angel presiding over the sphere of Sol.
semeroh		(meaning unknown).

Sendenna **Sondenna** **Sundenna**		name of an evil spirit.
ser		mourning, lamentation. Cf. *eophan.*
Shal **Shial**		angel powerful in transformation, ruled by *Aiaoai Oiiit.*
siaion **siaionu**	si-ay-on AC:C	temple, temples.
Sias		angel skilled in medicine, ruled by *Idoigo Ardza.* Also *Sigas.*
siasch	GD	= *esiasch,* brother.
siatris **skatarisa***	si-a-tris AC:C	scorpion, scorpions.
sibsi **sibesi**	sib-si AC:C	covenant.
Sigas		angel, also known as *Sias.*
Sigmorf		Governor of the First Division of the Aethyr *Tan.*
Sioda		Divine Name of Five Letters, ruling Earth of Fire.
Sisp **Siosp**		angel ruled by *Rzionr Nrzfm.*
skatarisa*	AC:C	= *siatris,* scorpion.
Slgaiol		Senior of Water, associated with Venus. Also *Lgaiol.*
smnad	smë-nad	another. Cf. *symp.*
Soageel		Governor of the Third Division of the Aethyr *Nia.*

Soaixnt		Senior of Water, associated
Soaiznt	AC:C	with Mercury.
soba	so-ba	whose, whom.
sobam	so-bam	
sobca	sob-ka	
sobol	so-bol	
sobra	so-bra	
sobha	so-ba	
soha	so-ha	
sobama	so-ba-ma	
sobame	AC:C, G	
sobeh-hah	GD	
sobola	AC:C	
sob-ha-atahe	AC:C	= *sobha ath,* whose works.
sobol	so-bol	west. (Also 'whose': see *soba*).
soboln	GD	
so-bolunu	AC:C	
bobanu*	AC:G	
bolanu*	AC:G	
sobra		= *soba,* whose.
sobrazod-ol	AC:C	= *sobra zol,* whose hands.
Sochial		Governor of the Third Division of the Aethyr *Lea.*
sola-bi-enu*	AC:G	= *solpeth bien,* hearken to my voice.
solamianu	AC:G	= *soba mian,* whose continuance.
solpeth	sol-peth	hearken, listen.
sol-petahe	AC:C	
Sondenna		= *Sendenna,* an evil spirit.
Sondn		Divine Name of Five Letters, ruling Water of Earth.

sonf **sonuf**	sonf AC:C	reign, rule.
sor		action.
soyga		will of God (?) (The *Book of Soyga* was one of Dee's holy books; the spirits said it was not a reversal of the Greek ἅγιοσ , holy.)
Spmnir		Divine Name of Six Letters, ruling Fire of Earth.
Srahpm		= *Lsrahpm,* Senior of Water.
Stim **Strim**		angel ruled by *Spmnir Llpiz.*
Stimcul		1) angel (Filius Lucis), associated with Saturn. 2) angel (Filia Filiarum Lucis) associated with Saturn.
Sudsamna		Kelley's good angel.
Sundenna		= *Sendenna,* an evil spirit.
surzas **surezodasa**	sur-zas AC:C	swear, be sworn. Cf. *zurza.*
symp	simp	another. Cf. *smnad.*

T Gisg 

t	ti	1) also. 2) it. 3) visit. Also *f*.
ta	ta	1) as. 2) thee (AC:G).
Taad		angel powerful in mixtures of natures, ruled by the angel *Ataad* and *Obgota Aabco*. Also *Taoad*. Companions are *Aadt, Adta, Dtaa*.
taba	ta-ba	govern. Also *caba*. Cf. *tabaan, tabaord*.
tabas	ta-bas	
tabaori	ta-bāri	
tabasa	AC:G	
tebasa	AC:G	
tabaan	ta-bān	governor. Cf. *taba, tabaord*.
tabaanu	AC:C	
tabaord	ta-bārd	govern, be governed.
tabaoreda	AC:C	
tabges	tab-jes	cave.
tabejesa	AC:C	
Tabitom		Governor of the Third Division of the Aethyr *Zax*.
Tahando		Governor of the Third Division of the Aethyr *Oxo*.
Tahaoeloj		Elemental King of Air.
tahil	AC:C	= *thil, thild, thiln,* seat.
tahila	AC:G	
tahilada	AC:C	
tahilanu	AC:C	

tal		name of the Enochian letter representing M.
talho	tal-ho	cup.
ta-labo*	AC:C	
taliobe	AC:C	= *tliob,* separate.
Tan		name of the Seventeenth Aethyr.
Taoad		angel, also known as *Taad.*
Taoagla		Governor of the First
Taongla	AC:C	Division of the Aethyr *Tex.*
Tapamal		Governor of the First Division of the Aethyr *Loe.*
tarananu	AC:C	= *tranan,* marrow.
tarianu	AC:C, G	= *trian,* shall be.
tarinuta	AC:C	= *trint,* sit.
tarofe	AC:C	= *trof,* building.
tasataxa	AC:C	= *tustax,* precede.
tastax	GD	
Tastoxo		Governor of the Third Division of the Aethyr *Oxo.*
tatan	ta-tan	wormwood.
tatanu	AC:C	
TAXS		7336.
tbl	ti-bël	= *tilb,* her.
Tdim		angel powerful in change of place, ruled by the angel *Atdim* and *Nelapr Omebb.* Companions are *Dimt, Imtd, Mtdi.*
Tdnim		

Teaa		Holy Name of Four Letters, ruling the Element of Fire.
Tedoand		Governor of the First Division of the Aethyr *Uta*.
Tedoond		
teloc	te-lok	death.
teloah	te-lo-a	
teloch	te-lok	
teloca	AC:C	
telocahe	AC:C, G	
telokake*	AC:G	
Tex		name of the Thirtieth Aethyr.
Thahaaotahe		Elemental King of Water.
thil	thil	seat, seats. Cf. *othil.*
thild	thild	
thiln	thiln	
tahil	AC:C	
tahila	AC:G	
tahilada	AC:C	
tahilanu	AC:C	
Thotanf		Governor of the First Division of the Aethyr *Paz.*
ti	GD	=*t i,* it is.
tia	ti-a	his.
tianta	ti-an-ta	bed.
tianuta	AC:C	
Tiarpax		Governor of the Third Division of the Aethyr *Lit.*
Tiiio		demonic name (reversal of *Oiiit*) commanding cacodemons of Earth of Air.
tibibp	ti-bib	sorrow.
tibibipe	AC:C	

tilb	tilb	her, of her.
tlb	tilb	
tiobl	ti-obl	
tilaba	AC:C	
tilabe	AC:C	
tibl	GD	
tiobela	AC:C	
tliob	të-li-ob	separate (v.)
taliobe	AC:C	
Toantom		Governor of the Second Division of the Aethyr *Asp*.
toatar	to-a-tar	hearken, listen. Cf. *solpeth*.
toatare	AC:C, G	
Tocarzi		Governor of the Third Division of the Aethyr *Tan*.
Toco		angel skilled in medicine, ruled by *Obgota Aabco*. Also *Togco*.
Todnaon		Governor of the Second Division of the Aethyr *Zid*.
tofglo	tof-glo	all things, everything. Cf. *tol*.
tofagilo	AC:G	
tofajilo	AC:G	
tofejilo	AC:C	
tofijilo	AC:G	
tofijila	AC:G	
tol glo	GD	
Togco		angel, also known as *Toco*.
toh	GD	see *homtoh*, triumph.
tohcoth		fairy, fairies (?)
Tohomaphala		name of a guardian angel.
Toitt		angel, also known as *Tott*.

tol	tol	all.
ton	ton	
tonu	AC:C	
tolahame	AC:C, G	= *tol ham,* all creatures.
toltorg	tol-torj	creature, creatures. Cf. *ham.*
toltorn	tol-torn	
tolteregi	AC:G	
toltoregi	AC:C, G	
toltoreji	AC:G	
toltorenu	AC:C	
tore-torenu	AC:C	
toltorgi	GD	
ton		= *tol,* all.
tonug	to-nug	deface, be defaced.
tonuji	AC:C	
tooat	to-wat	furnish, provide. Cf. *abraasa.*
tooata	AC:C	
Tor		Name of the Twenty-Third Aethyr.
torezodu	AC:C	= *torzu, torzul, torzulp,* arise.
torezodul	AC:C	
torezodulape	AC:C	
torgi	GD	see *toltorg,* creature.
torgu		= *torzu,* arise.
Torzoxi		Governor of the First Division of the Aethyr *Pop.*
torzu	tor-zu	arise.
torgu	tor-ju	
torzul	tor-zul	
tor-zulp	tor-zulp	
torezodu	AC:C	
torezodul	AC:C	
torezodulape	AC:C	

Totocan		Governor of the Third Division of the Aethyr *Chr.*
Tott		angel skilled in medicine, ruled by *Idoigo Ardza.* Also *Toitt.*
tox	tox	of him, his. Cf. *tia.*
totza	AC:G	
toxa	AC:C	
Tpau		angel, companion of *Utpa.*
Tplau		
Tplabc		demonic name (reversal of *Cbalpt*) commanding cacodemons of Earth of Earth.
tranan	tra-nan	marrow.
tarananu	AC:C	
trian	tri-an	shall be.
tarianu	AC:C, G	
trint	trint	sit.
tarinuta	AC:C	
trof	trof	building. Cf. *orsca.*
tarofe	AC:C	
turbs	turbz	beauty.
turebesa	AC:C, G	
tustax	tus-tax	go before, precede.
tastax	GD	
tasataxa	AC:C	

U/V Van

Word	Pronunciation / Source	Meaning
Vaa		name of an angel who appeared to Dee and Kelley ('Scourge of those who resist the power, will and command of God').
Vaasa		angel, also known as *Vasa.*
vabzir	vab-zir	eagle.
vabezodire	AC:C	
Vadali		Divine Name of Six Letters, ruling Water of Fire.
valasa	AC:G	= *uls,* end.
Valgars		Governor of the Third Division of the Aethyr *Lil.*
vamuela	AC:G	= *uml,* add.
van		name of the Enochian letter representing V.
vau	GD	
Vanarda	AC:C	= *Usnarda,* Governor.
vanucahi	AC:C	= *unchi,* confound.
vanupehe	AC:G	= *unph,* anger.
vaoan	vau-an	truth. Cf. *vooan.*
vaoanu	AC:G, GD	
vaomesareji	AC:C	= *vomsarg,* every one of you.
vaoresa	AC:C	= *vors,* over.
vaoresaji	AC:C, G	= *vors g,* over you.
vaoresagi	AC:G	
vaorsag	GD	
vaorsagi	GD	
varanu	AC:C	= *uran,* elder.

Vasa		angel ruled by *Iaaasd Atapa.* Also *Vaasa.*
Vasg **Varsg**		angel skilled in medicine, ruled by *Noalmr Oloag.*
Vastrim		Governor of the First Division of the Aethyr *Rii.*
vau	GD	=*van,* Enochian letter.
vaugeji	AC:C, G	=*ugeg,* wax strong.
vaukaho*	AC:G	=*unchi,* confound.
vaul **vaun** **vaunu** **vavale**	vaul vaun AC:C AC:C	work (v.)
vaulasa	AC:C	=*uls,* end.
vaun		=*vaul,* work.
vaunala	AC:C	=*unalab,* skirt.
vaunesa*	AC:C, G	=*unal,* these.
vaunigilaji **vaunilaji** **vaunilagi**	AC:C AC:G AC:G	=*uniglag,* descend.
vaunud-el	AC:C	=*undl,* remainder.
vaunupehe	AC:C	=*unph, vonph,* anger.
vaunupeho	AC:C	=*vonpho,* anger.
vaupaahe	AC:C	=*upaah,* wing.
vaurebes	AC:C	=*urbs,* beautify.
vaurelar*	AC:C	=*urelp,* seething.
Vavaamp		Governor of the Second Division of the Aethyr *Maz.*
vavale	AC:C	=*vaul,* work.

vax	AC:C	= *VX*, 42.
ucim	u-sim	frown not (smile?).
vcim	GD	
ucime	AC:C	
veh		name of the Enochian letter representing C.
velucorsapax	AC:VV	enthroned.
vep	vep	flame. Cf. *ialprg*.
vepe	AC:C	
ugear	u-jar	strength. Cf. *ugeg*.
vgear	GD	
ujeare	AC:C	
ugeg	u-jej	wax strong, grow strong.
ugegi	u-je-ji	
vgeg	GD	
vgegi	GD	
vaugeji	AC:C, G	
vicap		(meaning unknown).
vi-i-v	GD	= *viu*, second.
vi-i-vau	AC:C	
vi-i-vl	GD	= *viu l*, second of the first.
uime	AC:C	see *vovim*, dragon.
vime*	AC:G	= *unph*, wrath.
vinu	AC:G	invoke.
uirequo	AC:C	= *virq*, nest.
Virooli		Governor of the Second Division of the Aethyr *Zom*.
virq	virk	nest.
uirequo	AC:C	
viruden	AC:VV	beautified. Cf. *urbs*.

viu	vi-u	second.
viv	AC:C, GD	
vi-i-v	GD	
u-i-v	GD	
vi-vau	AC:C	
viviala pereta	AC:C	= *viu ialprt,* second flame.
vi-vi-iv	GD	= *viu diu,* second angle.
Vivipos		Governor of the Second Division of the Aethyr *Uta.*
Vixpalg		Governor of the Third Division of the Aethyr *Asp.*
ujeare	AC:C	= *ugear,* strength.
ulcinin	ul-si-nin	happy.
vlcinina	GD	
il ci ninu*	AC:C	
uls	uls	end, ends.
vls	GD	
vaulasa	AC:C	
um		= *umd,* called.
umadea	u-ma-de-a	tower.
vmadea	GD	
vo-ma-dea	AC:C	
umapelifa	AC:C	= *umplif,* strength.
umd	umd	call, be called.
um	um	
uml	um-ël	add.
vml	GD	
umela	AC:C	
umplif	um-plif	strength. Cf. *ugear.*
vmplif	GD	
umapelifa	AC:C	

un		name of the Enochian letter representing A.
unal	u-nal	these, those.
vnal	GD	
vaunala	AC:C	
unalah	u-na-lā	skirt, skirts.
vnalah	GD	
vaunalahe	AC:C	
uncal		(meaning unknown).
unchi	un-chi	confound. Cf. *oucho*.
vnchi	GD	
vanucahi	AC:C	
vaukaho*	AC:G	
undl	un-dël	remainder, rest
vnd-l	GD	
vaunud-el	AC:C	
unig	u-nig	require.
vnig	GD	
uniji	AC:C	
uniglag	u-nig-lag	descend, go down. Cf. *arphe*.
vniglag	GD	
vaunigilaji	AC:C	
vaunilaji	AC:G	
vaunilagi	AC:G	
Unnax		Divine Name of Five Letters, ruling Air of Earth.
unph	unf	anger, wrath. Also *vonph*.
vnph	GD	
vanupehe	AC:G	
vaunupehe	AC:C	
vo	AC:VV	wherein.
vohim	vo-him	mighty. Cf. *canse, micalz*.
vohima	AC:C	

vo-ma-dea	AC:C	=*umadea,* tower.
vomsarg	vom-sarj	every one of you. Cf. *g.*
vaomesareji	AC:C	
vomesareji	AC:G	
vonsarg	GD	
vonph	vonf	anger, wrath. Cf. *unph.*
vonpho	von-fo	
vaunupehe	AC:C	
vaunupeho	AC:C	
vonupehe	AC:C	
vonsarg	GD	=*vomsarg,* every one of you.
vooan	vō-an	truth. Cf. *vaoan.* (*Vooan* is the pronunciation used by the fallen angels.)
vooanu	AC:G	
vors	vorz	over.
voresa	AC:G	
vaoresa	AC:C	
vorsag	AC:G, GD	=*vors g,* over you.
vovim	vo-vim	dragon.
vovin	vo-vin	
vovina	vo-vi-na	
uo uime	AC:C, G	
upaah	u-pā	wing, wings.
upaahi	u-pā-hi	
upaahe	AC:C	
vpaah	GD	
vpaahi	GD	
vaupaahe	AC:C	
ur		name of the Enochian letter representing L.
uran	u-ran	1) see. 2) elder, elders. Also *gran.*
vran	GD	
varanu	AC:C	

urbs	urbz	beautify. Cf. *turbs*.
vrbs	GD	
vaurebes	AC:C	
Urch		confounding angels.
urelp	u-relp	seething.
vrelp	GD	
vaurelar*	AC:C	
Urzla		=*Erzla,* angel.
Usnarda		Governor of the Second
Vanarda	AC:C	Division of the Aethyr *Ich*.
Ussn		angel skilled in finding metals
Uspsn		and precious stones, ruled by *Nelapr Omebb*.
Uta		name of the Fourteenth
Vta	AC:C, GD	Aethyr.
Uti		name of the Twenty-Fifth
Vti	AC:C, GD	Aethyr.
Utpa		angel powerful in change of
Utlpa		place, ruled by the angel *Eutpa* and *Llacza Palam*. Companions are *Tpau, Paut, Autp*.
VX		42.
vax	AC:C	

X Pal

Xai cacodemon, counterpart of the angel *Aira.*

Xannu demonic name (reversal of *Unnax*) commanding cacodemons of Air of Earth.

Xcz cacodemon, counterpart of the angel *Czns.*

Xda cacodemon, counterpart of the angel *Dapi.*

Xgzd
Xgazd angel powerful in finding out secrets of men, ruled by the angel *Hxgzd* and *Aourrz Aloai.* Companions are *Gzdx, Zdxg, Dxgz.*

Xii cacodemon, counterpart of the angel *Iipo.*

Xnlr
Xnilr angel, companion of *Nlrx.*

Xom cacodemon, counterpart of the angel *Omgg.*

Xoo cacodemon, counterpart of the angel *Oopz.*

Xoy cacodemon, counterpart of the angel *Oyub.*

Xpa cacodemon, counterpart of the angel *Pali.*

Xpcn
Xpacn angel ruled by *Iaaasd Atapa.*

Xrnh
Xrinh angel powerful in transformation, ruled by *Maladi Olaad.*

Z Ceph

z	zë	they.
zod	AC:C	
Za		name of an angel who appeared to Dee and Kelley ('Transmitter of Gifts').
Zaa		name of the Twenty-Seventh Aethyr.
Zabo		angel, companion of *Boza.*
Zaabo		
zacam	za-kam	move.
zacar	za-kar	
zacare	za-ka-re	
zodaca	AC:G	
zodacame	AC:C	
zodakame	AC:G	
zodacar	GD	
zodacara	GD	
zodakara	AC:C	
zodacare	AC:C	
zodakare	AC:C	
zodame*	AC:G	
Zadzaczadlin		Adam (in the language of the *Book of Soyga).*
Zafasai		Governor of the Second Division of the Aethyr *Zen.*
Zamfres		Governor of the First
Zainfres	AC:C	Division of the Aethyr *Zid.*
zamran	zam-ran	appear, show oneself.
zodamerann*	AC:G	
zodameranu	AC:C, G	
zodamran	GD	

zar **zodare**	zar AC:C	course, courses. Cf. *elzap*.
Zarnaah		angelic King ruling in the North.
Zarzi		angel, also known as *Zazi*.
Zarzilg		angelic King ruling in the East-South-East.
Zax		name of the Tenth Aethyr.
Zaxanin		Governor of the Third Division of the Aethyr *Tor*.
Zazi		angel, companion of *Ziza*. Also *Zarzi*.
Zdxg **Zdaxg**		angel, companion of *Xgzd*.
Zedekiel		planetary angel presiding over the sphere of Jupiter.
Zen		name of the Eighteenth Aethyr.
Zibra		demonic name (reversal of *Arbiz*) commanding cacodemons of Earth of Earth.
Zid		name of the Eighth Aethyr.
zien **zodien**	zīn AC:C	hand, hands. Cf. *zol, ozien, ozol*.
zil	zil	stretch forth (?) See *Zilodarp*.
zildar **zodiladare**	zil-dar AC:C	fly, flew.
Zildron		Governor of the First Division of the Aethyr *Chr*.
Zilodarp **Zodilodarepe**	zil-od-arp AC:C	a name of God: 'Stretch-Forth-and-Conquer'.

Zim		name of the Thirteenth Aethyr.
zimii	zi-mī	enter.
zodimii	AC:C	
zimz	zimz	vestures; apparel, clothing. Cf. *oboleh, qaa.*
zodimezod	AC:C	
zodimezoda	AC:G	
Zinggen		angelic King ruling in the West-North-West.
Zip		name of the Ninth Aethyr.
Zipll		demonic name (reversal of *Llpiz*) commanding cacodemons of Fire of Earth.
zir		presence.
zir	zir	I am.
zirdo	zir-do	
zire	GD	
zodir	AC:C, G	
zodiredo	AC:C, G	
zodireda	AC:VV	
zodivedo*	AC:G	
Ziracah		angelic King ruling in the South.
zirdo		= *zir,* I am.
zire	GD	
Zirenaiad		a name of God: 'I am the Lord your God' (Zir Enay Iad).
zirn	zirn	wonder, wonders (n.) Cf. *sald.*
zodirenu	AC:C	
zirom	zi-rom	was, were.
zirop	zi-rop	
zodirome	AC:C	
zodirope	AC:C	

Zirza		angel, also known as *Ziza.*
Zirzird		Governor of the Third Division of the Aethyr *Maz.*
Ziza		angel powerful in finding out secrets of men, ruled by the angel *Pziza* and *Rzionr Nrzfm.* Also *Zirza.* Companions are *Izaz, Zazi, Aziz.*
Zod-ee-zod-ah	GD	
zizop	zi-zop	vessel, container.
zodizodope	AC:C	
Zlar		angel, companion of *Rzla.*
Zliar		
zlida	zli-da	water (v.)
zode-lide	AC:C	
zna		motion, movement.
znurza	znur-za	swear, swore. Cf. *surzas.*
zurza	zur-za	
znrza	GD	
zodenurezoda	AC:C	
zod	AC:C	= *z,* they.
zodaca	AC:G	= *zacam, zacar, zacare,* move.
zodacame	AC:C	
zodakame	AC:G	
zodacar	GD	
żodacara	GD	
zodakare	AC:C	
zodakara	AC:C	
zodameta	AC:G	conjure thee.
zodamran	GD	= *zamran,* appear.
zodare	AC:C	= *zar,* course.
zodayolana	AC:C	= *zylna,* itself.

Zod-ee-zod-ah		=*Ziza,* an angel.
zode-lida	AC:C	=*zlida,* water.
zodenurezoda	AC:C	=*znurza,* swear.
zodien	AC:C	=*zien,* hand.
zodiladare	AC:C	=*zildar,* fly.
Zodilodarepe	AC:C	=*Zilodarp,* 'Stretch-forth-and-Conquer': a name of God.
zodimezod	AC:C	=*zimz,* vestures.
zodimezoda	AC:G	
zodimibe	AC:G	veil.
zodimii	AC:C	=*zimii,* enter.
zodinu	AC:G	water. Cf. *zlida.*
zodir	AC:C, G	=*zir, zirdo,* I am.
zodiredo	AC:C, G	
zodireda	AC:VV	inhabit.
zodirenu	AC:C	=*zirn,* wonder.
zodirome	AC:C	=*zirom, zirop,* were.
zodirope	AC:C	
zodivedo*	AC:G	=*zirdo,* I am.
zodixalayo	AC:C	=*zixlay,* stir up.
zodizodarasa	AC:G	=*balzizras,* judgment.
zodizodearasa	AC:G	
zodizodope	AC:C	=*zizop,* vessel.
zodomeda	AC:C	=*zomd,* midst.
zodonace	AC:C	=*zonac,* apparelled.
zodonugonu	AC:C, G	=*zong,* wind.
zodonurenusagi	AC:C	=*zonrensg,* deliver.

zodoreje	AC:C, G	= *zorge,* be friendly.
zodumebi	AC:C, G	= *zumvi,* sea.
zol	zol	hand. Cf. *zien.*
Zom		name of the Third Aethyr.
zomd	zomd	midst.
zodomeda	AC:C	
zonac	zo-nak	apparelled, dressed, clothed.
zodonace	AC:C	
zong	zong	wind.
zodonugonu	AC:C, G	
zonrensg	zon-renj	deliver. Cf. *obelisong.*
zodonurenusagi	AC:C	
zorge	zorj	be friendly.
zodoreje	AC:C, G	
Zrruoa		demonic name (reversal of *Aourrz*) commanding cacodemons of Fire of Air.
zudna		(meaning unknown).
zuraah		fervently, with humility.
zurah		
Zurchol		angelic King ruling in the South-South-East.
zure		(meaning unknown).
zurza	zur-za	= *znurza,* swear.
zylna	zil-na	itself.
zodayolana	AC:C	

Explicit Thesaurus Linguae Angelorum

PART II

ENGLISH — ANGELIC

English	*Angelic*

A

abiding	**cafafam**
ability	**bab**
able — *see* can	
abode	**cafafam**
according to	**marb**
action	**sor**
Adam	**Zadzaczadlin**
add	**uml**
admiration	**rsam**
Aethyrs (numbers indicate the order of the Aethyrs)	**Arn** *2* **Asp** *21* **Bag** *28* **Chr** *20* **Deo** *7* **Des** *26* **Ich** *11* **Lea** *16* **Lil** *1* **Lin** *22* **Lit** *5* **Loe** *12* **Maz** *6* **Nia** *24* **Oxo** *15* **Paz** *4* **Pop** *19* **Rii** *29* **Tan** *17* **Tex** *30* **Tor** *23* **Uta** *14* **Uti** *25* **Zaa** *27* **Zax** *10* **Zen** *18* **Zid** *8* **Zim** *13* **Zip** *9* **Zom** *3*
age	**homin**
Air (Element):	
— Spirit:	**Exarp**
— Holy Names ruling:	**Oro Ibah Aozpi**
— Divine Names ruling sub-elements:	
Air of Air	**Idoigo Ardza**
Earth of Air	**Aiaoai Oiiit**

Fire of Air	**Aourrz Aloai**
Water of Air	**Llacza Palam**
— Demonic Names ruling sub-elements:	
Air of Air	**Ogiodi Azdra**
Earth of Air	**Iaoaia Tiiio**
Fire of Air	**Zrruao Iaola**
Water of Air	**Azcall Malap**
— Seniors (with planetary associations):	
Sol (Elemental King)	**Bataivah**
Luna	**Htmorda**
Mars	**Habioro**
Mercury	**Acmbicu**
Jupiter	**Aaoxaif**
Venus	**Ahaozpi**
Saturn	**Hipotga**
— Great Elemental King:	**Tahaoeloj**
all	**tol, ton**
All-Powerful (title of God)	**Iaidon**
all things	**tofglo**
also	**t**
always	**paid**
am — *see* be	
amidst	**nothoa**
among	**aaf, aai, aao, eai, oai, nothoa**
and	**od; sa** (AC:G)
angels (names of) — minor angels	**Aaan Aadt Aana Aanaa Aaodt Aavan Aavna Abamo Abaoz Abmo**

— minor angels (continued)	**Aboz Acar Acca Acps Acrar Acuca Acups Adire Adnop Adop Adopa Adota Adre Adta Aglm Agmlm Aigra Aira Amox Amsox Anaa Ancro Anro Anvaa Aomi Aosmi Apahr Aphr Aplst Apst Arizl Arzl Ataad Atdim Aultp Autp Axir Axtir Aziz Azriz Boaza Boza Bracn Brap Brcn Briap Cnabr Cnbr Cpsa Cpusa Czns Czons Daltt Dapi Daspi Datt Diari Dimt Dinmt Diom Diri Dixom Dolop Donpa Doop Dopa Dtaa Dtoaa Dxagz Dxgz Eboza Ecaop Ecop Ephra Erzla Eutpa Faax Fatax Fmnd Fmond Gbal Gbeal Glma Glmma Gmdnm Gzadx Gzdx Hcnbr Hiaom Hraap Hrap Hroan Hxgzd Iaba Iahl Iamhl Ianba Iaom Iasom Iidpo Iipo Imntd Imtd Izaz Izinr Izixp Iznr Izraz Izxp Lairz Larz Leaoc Leoc Lmag Lmmag Lrixn Lrxn Magl Magm Mamgl Masgm Miao Misao Msal Msmal Mtdi Mtndi Naaa Naoo Naooo Navaa Nbarc Nbrc Ndazn Ndzn Nhdd**

— minor angels (continued)

Nhodd Nlirx Nlrx Npat
Nrcoa Nroa Oacnr Oanr
Ocanm Ocnm Omagg
Omgg Omia Omsia
Oodpz Oopz Opad
Opamn Opmn Opana
Opna Opnad Ormn
Orpmn Otoi Otroi
Oyaub Oyub Ozaab
Ozab Paco Pado Paeoc
Palco Pali Palut Pando
Panli Paoc Paut Phara
Phra Pmagl Pmox
Pmzox Ppsac Psac
Psuac Pziza Raaph
Raph Rbnh Rbznh
Rcanb Rcnb Rgan
Rgoan Rlemu Rlmu
Roan Rocan Rsoni Rsni
Ruoi Ruroi Rxao Rxinl
Rxnl Rxpao Rzila Rzla
Saaiz Sacp Saiz Saucp
Scio Scmio Shal Shial
Sias Sigas Siosp Sisp
Stim Strim Taad Taoad
Tdim Tdnim Toco Togco
Toitt Tott Tpau Tplau
Vaasa Vasa Uspsn Ussn
Utlpa Utpa Xgazd Xgzd
Xnilr Xpaxn Xpcn Xrinh
Xrnh Zaabo Zabo Zarzi
Zazi Zdaxg Zdxg Zirza
Ziza

— planetary angels, with associated planets (see page 27):

	angel of sphere	Filiae Lucis	Filii Lucis	Filiae Filiarum Lucis	Filii Filiorum Lucis
Sol	*Semeliel*	**El (L)**	**I**	**S**	**E**
Luna	*Levanael*	**Me**	**Ih**	**Ab**	**An**
Venus	*Nogahel*	**Ese**	**Ilr**	**Ath**	**Ave**
Jupiter	*Zedekiel*	**Iana**	**Dmal**	**Ized**	**Liba**
Mars	*Madimiel*	**Akele**	**Heeoa**	**Ekiei**	**Rocle**
Mercury	*Corabiel*	**Azdobn**	**Beigia**	**Madimi**	**Hagonel**
Saturn	*Sabathiel*	**Stimcul**	**Stimcul**	**Esemeli**	**Ilemese**

— orders of angels:

confirming angels	**Sach**
confounding angels	**Urch**
ministering angels	**Lang**
praising angels	**Luah**

— angelic Kings, with region in which ruling:

East	**Olpaged**
East-South-East	**Zarzilg**
South-South-East	**Zurchol**
South	**Ziracah**
South-South-West	**Lavavoth**
West-South-West	**Alpudus**
West	**Hononol**
West-North-West	**Zinggen**
North-North-West	**Cadaamp**
North	**Zarnaah**
North-North-East	**Arfaolg**
East-North-East	**Gebabal**

— other angels and good spirits:

Aflafben
Bamasan
Ben
Corfax
Ga

	Galvah
	Iubanladaec
	Lasben
	Mapsama
	Murifri
	Nalvage
	Obelison
	Phanael
	Sudsamna
	Tohomaphala
	Vaa
	Za
— see also Governors, Kings, Princes, Seniors	
anger	**unph, vonph, vonpho**
angle	**diu**
another	**symp, smnad, ca**
any	**droln**
apparel — *see also* garments, vestures	**zimz**
apparelled	**zonac**
appear	**zamran**
apply oneself	**imvamar**
are — *see* be	
arise	**torzu, torzul, torzulp, torgu**
ark	**erm**
art (thou art) — *see* be	

as	**ca, ta**
— even as	**nomig**
as many	**plosi**
avoidance of earthly things	**nalvage**

B

Babes of the Abyss (?)	**gaha** (AC: VV)
balance (n.)	**prap**
be	
— I am	**zir, zirdo**
— thou art	**geh**
— he/she/it is	**i**
— they are	**chiis, chis, chiso**
— was	**as, zirop**
— it was (?)	**nostoah**
— were	**zirom**
— shall be	**trian**
— let there be	**christeos**
— be thou!	**bolp**
— is not	**ipam**
— cannot be	**ipamis**
— be (become)	**noan, noaln, noar, noas, noasmi; nenni** (AC: VV)
be friendly	**zorge**
be mighty	**omicaolz**
beast (of the field)	**levithmong**
beautify	**urbs; viruden** (AC: VV)
beauty	**turbs**
because	**bagle, baglen**
— *see also* therefore, wherefore	
become	**noan, noaln, noar, noas, noasmi**
bed	**tianta**
before	**aspt**
— go before	**tustax**

begin anew	**amgedpha**
beginning	**acroodzi, croodzi, gevamna, iaod, ioadaf**
begotten	**gedotbar**
behold	**micma**
bind up	**allar**
bitter sting	**grosb**
blood	**cnila**
branch	**lilonon**
breath	**gigipah**
brightness	**luciftian, luciftias**
bring down	**drix**
bring forth	**yolcam, yolci**
brother	**esiasch**
buckler	**lolcis**
building	**orsca, trof**
built	**on** (AC: VV)
burn	**ialpon**
burning	**ialpor**
but	**crip, crp, oq**

C

cacodemons — *see* demons	
call (be called)	**umd, um**
can (be able to)	**adgt**
carry out (execute)	**fifis**
cast down	**adrpan**
cattle	**levithmong**
cave	**tabges**
centre	**ovoars**
chamber	**ooge**
circle	**comselh**
clothed	**zonac**
clothes, clothing — *see also* garments, vestures	**zimz**
coat	**mabza**
come, come away, come forth	**niis, niisa, niiso**
come out	**carma**
comfort (n.)	**blior, bliar, bliora, bliorb, bliors, bliort, bliard**
comfort (v.)	**bliorax**
comforter	**bigliad**
conclude (include)	**iaial**
confirming angels	**Sach**
confound	**oucho, unchi**

confounding angels	**Urch**
conjure thee	**zodameta** (AC: G)
container	**izizop, zizop**
contents	**q**
continually	**pild**
continuance	**miam, mian, nuam**
conquer (?)	**arp**
corner	**miinoag**
count	**cormp, cormpo, cormpt**
course	**elzap; zar** (AC: C)
covenant	**sibsi**
cover	**ethamz**
creation	**qaa, qaan, qaaon, qaas**
creator	**qaal, qadah**
creature	**ham, hami, toltorg, toltorn**
crown (n.)	**momao**
crown (v.)	**momar**
crucible (?)	**rlodnr**
cry aloud	**bahal**
cup	**talbo**
curse	**amma**

D

dark heavens	**mahorela** (AC: VV)
darkness	**ors**
daughter	**pasbs**
day	**basgim**
— midday	**bazm**
death	**teloc, teloch, teloah**
deed	**gru**
deface (be defaced)	**tonug**
deliver	**zonrensg**
deliverer	**obelisong**
demons, names of:	
— cacodemons	**Aax Adi Agb And Aor Apa Apm Ash Asi Ast Ato Ava Cab Cac Cam Cms Cop Csc Cus Eac Erg Ern Exr Hbr Hru Hua Mgm Miz Mma Moc Mop Mto Oap Odo Oec Oia Ona Onh Onp Pdi Pfm Pia Piz Rad Rda Rpa Rrb Rrl Rsi Rxp Xai Xcz Xdz Xii Xom Xoy Xpa**
— other demons and evil spirits:	**Adraman** **Arzulgh** **Barma** **Belmagel** **Coronzon** **Ganislay** **Githgulcag**

	Orh
	Paulacarp
— demonic names (commanding demons of sub-elements):	
Air of Air	**Ogiodi Azdra**
Earth of Air	**Iaoaia Tiiio**
Fire of Air	**Zrruoa Iaola**
Water of Air	**Azcall Malap**
Air of Earth	**Iopgna Xannu**
Earth of Earth	**Tplabc Zibra**
Fire of Earth	**Rinmps Zipll**
Water of Earth	**Meeana Ndnos**
Air of Fire	**Rmlaon Gaolo**
Earth of Fire	**Odxlov Adois**
Fire of Fire	**Rnoizr Mfzrn**
Water of Fire	**Iladav Avabo**
Air of Water	**Atogbo Ocbaa**
Earth of Water	**Idalam Daalo**
Fire of Water	**Dsaaai Apata**
Water of Water	**Rpalen Bbemo**
descend	**uniglag, arphe**
destroy	**quasb**
diamond	**childao**
differ	**dilzmo**
diminish	**prdzar**
discord	**osf**
dispose	**lrasd**
divide	**poilp**
Divine and Holy Names — of elements:	
Air	**Oro Ibah Aozpi**
Earth	**Mor Dial Hctga**

Fire	**Oip Teaa Pdoce**
Water	**Mph Arsl Gaiol**
— of sub-elements:	
Air of Air	**Idoigo Ardza**
Earth of Air	**Aiaoai Oiiit**
Fire of Air	**Aourrz Aloai**
Water of Air	**Llacza Palam**
Air of Earth	**Angpoi Unnax**
Earth of Earth	**Cbalpt Arbiz**
Fire of Earth	**Spmnir Llpiz**
Water of Earth	**Anaeem Sondn**
Air of Fire	**Noalmr Oloag**
Earth of Fire	**Volxdo Sioda**
Fire of Fire	**Rzionr Nrzfm**
Water of Fire	**Vadali Obava**
Air of Water	**Obgota Aabco**
Earth of Water	**Maladi Olaad**
Fire of Water	**Iaaasd Atapa**
Water of Water	**Nelapr Omebb**
divine knowledge	**iadnah, iadnamad**
division	**yrpoil**
do, does	**gnay**
dragon	**vovim, vovin, vovina**
dressed	**zonac**
drunken	**orsba**
dryness	**orscor**
duke	**oheloka** (AC: G)
dwell — *see also* live	**faonts, praf, pragma**
dwelling, dwelling-place — *see also* house, building	**faorgt, fargt, paradial**

E

eagle	**vabzir**
Earth (Element):	
— Spirit:	**Nanta**
— Holy Names ruling:	**Mor Dial Hctga**
— Divine Names ruling sub-elements:	
Air of Earth	**Angpoi Unnax**
Earth of Earth	**Cbalpt Arbiz**
Fire of Earth	**Spmnir Llpiz**
Water of Earth	**Anaeem Sondn**
— Demonic Names ruling sub-elements:	
Air of Earth	**Iopgna Xannu**
Earth of Earth	**Tplabc Zibra**
Fire of Earth	**Rinmps Zipll**
Water of Earth	**Meeana Ndnos**
— Seniors (with planetary associations):	
Sol (Elemental King)	**Iczhhcal**
Luna	**Lzinopo**
Mars	**Laidrom**
Mercury	**Acmbicu**
Jupiter	**Aczinor**
Venus	**Alhctga**
Saturn	**Liiansa**
— Great Elemental King:	**Thahaaotahe**
east	**raas, raasy**
echoing	**matorb**
eight	**p**
elder	**gran, uran**

Elemental Kings:	
— Air	**Tahaoeloj;** **Bataivah** (Senior)
— Earth	**Thahaaotahe;** **Iczhhcal** (Senior)
— Fire	**Ohooohaatan;** **Edelprna** (Senior)
— Water	**Thahebyobeeatan;** **Raagiosl** (Senior)
elevated	**ofekufa** (AC:VV)
empty	**affa**
end	**uls, galvah**
Enochian letters:	**Ceph** Z **Don** R **Drux** N **Fam** S **Gal** D **Ged** G/J **Ger** Q **Gisg** T **Gon** I/Y **Graph** E **Mals** P **Med** O **Na** H **Or** F **Pa** B **Pal** X **Tal** M **Un** A **Ur** L **Van** U/V **Veh** C/K
enter	**zimii**

enthroned — *see also* throne	**velucorsapax**
entire	**saga**
equal	**parach**
even as	**nomig**
everlasting	**gohed**
everything	**tofglo**
evil spirits — *see* demons	
except	**m**
execute (carry out)	**fifis**
exist — existed — will exist — *see also* be	**gahal** (AC:VV) **gaha** (AC:VV) **gahalana** (AC:VV)
eye	**ooanoan, ooaona**

F

face	**adoian**
fact	**gru**
faith	**gono**
fall	**dobix, loncho**
fasten	**amizpi**
fear (n.)	**hoxmarch**
feet — *see* foot	
fervently	**zuraah, zurah**
fiery darts	**malprg, malpirgi**
fire	**malprg, malpirgi, prge, prgel**
Fire (Element):	
— Spirit:	**Bitom**
— Holy Names ruling:	**Oip Teaa Pdoce**
— Divine Names ruling sub-elements:	
Air of Fire	**Noalmr Oloag**
Earth of Fire	**Volxdo Sioda**
Fire of Fire	**Rzionr Nrzfm**
Water of Fire	**Vadali Obava**
— Demonic Names ruling sub-elements:	
Air of Fire	**Rmlaon Gaolo**
Earth of Fire	**Odxlov Adois**
Fire of Fire	**Rnoizr Mfzrn**
Water of Fire	**Idalav Avabo**
— Seniors (with planetary associations):	
Sol (Elemental King)	**Edelprna**

Luna	**Asndood**
Mars	**Aaetpio**
Mercury	**Anodoin**
Jupiter	**Adoeoct**
Venus	**Aapdoce**
Saturn	**Arinnap**
— Great Elemental King	**Ohooohaatan**
firmament	**calz**
firmament of waters	**pilzin**
first	**el, elo, l, la, li, lo**
five	**o**
flame	**ialprg, ialprt, vep**
flames (of first glory)	**ialpirgah**
flaming	**ialpor**
flourish	**cacacom**
flower	**lorslq**
fly (v.)	**zildar**
follower	**fafen**
foot	**lasdi, lusd, lusda**
for (because)	**lap**
forget	**bams**
four, fourth	**s, es**
frame (v.)	**izazaz**
friendly (be friendly)	**zorge**
front (in front of)	**aspt**
frown not	**ucim**
furnace (?)	**rlodnr**
furnish (provide)	**tooat**
fury	**bagie**

G

garland	**obloc**
garment — *see also* apparel, vestures	**oboleh, qaa**
garnish	**gnonp**
gather	**aldon**
gathering	**aldi**
gird	**aldon**
girdle	**atraah**
give, given	**dluga, dlugam, dlugar, phamah**
glory	**busd, busdir, adgmach**
go before	**tustax**
go down	**uniglag**
God	**Ascha, Iabes, Iad, Mad, Oiad, Piad**
God (names of):	**Baeovib, Gahoachma, Iadpil, Iaida, Iaidon, Idoian** (AC:VV), **Idoigo, Ioiad, L, Zilodarp, Zirenaiad**
gold	**audcal**
govern	**caba, taba**
govern (be governed)	**tabaord**
government	**netaab, netaaib, netab**
governor	**tabaan**
Governors of Aethyrs:	**Abaiond** 2/Pop **Advorpt** 3/Tex

— Governors of Aethyrs (continued)	**Ambriol**	**3/Loe**
	Andispi	**3/Zom**
	Aspiaon	**3/Deo**
	Axziarg	**2/Pax**
	Aydropl	**2/Tan**
	Bazchim	**3/Des**
	Calzirg	**3/Lin**
	Chialps	**2/Nia**
	Chirspa	**1/Asp**
	Comanan	**2/Zax**
	Cralpir	**2/Zip**
	Cucarpt	**1/Lea**
	Dialiva	**3/Arn**
	Doagnis	**1/Arn**
	Doanzin	**3/Zip**
	Docepax	**3/Zim**
	Dozinal	**4/Tex**
	Focisni	**2/Bag**
	Gecaond	**1/Zim**
	Gedoons	**2/Loe**
	Gemnimb	**2/Tex**
	Genadol	**2/Deo**
	Gomziam	**3/Rii**
	Yalpamb	**3/Zen**
	Labnixp	**1/Bag**
	Laparin	**2/Zim**
	Lavacon	**2/Lea**
	Lazdixi	**1/Lit**
	Lexarph	**1/Zax**
	Mathula	**2/Zaa**
	Mirzind	**1/Uti**
	Molpand	**1/Ich**
	Nabaomi	**1/Zen**
	Nigrana	**2/Des**
	Nocamal	**2/Lit**
	Nociabi	**2/Oxo**
	Obmacas	**1/Deo**
	Obvaors	**2/Uti**
	Occodon	**1/Lil**

— Governors of Aethyrs (continued)	**Oddiorg**	**1/Zip**
	Odraxti	**2/Rii**
	Omagrap	**3/Pop**
	Onizimp	**2/Tor**
	Ooanamb	**3/Uta**
	Orcanin	**1/Nia**
	Orpanib	**3/Zaa**
	Oxlopar	**3/Bag**
	Ozidaia	**1/Lin**
	Pacasna	**2/Arn**
	Paraoan	**2/Lin**
	Parziba	**2/Chr**
	Pascomb	**2/Lil**
	Ponodol	**3/Ich**
	Pophand	**1/Des**
	Pothnir	**3/Paz**
	Pristac	**3/Zid**
	Ranglam	**3/Uti**
	Ronoamb	**1/Tor**
	Samapha	**1/Zom**
	Saxtomp	**1/Maz**
	Saziami	**1/Zaa**
	Sigmorf	**1/Tan**
	Soageel	**3/Nia**
	Sochial	**3/Lea**
	Tabitom	**3/Zax**
	Tahando	**1/Oxo**
	Taoagla	**1/Tex**
	Tapamal	**1/Loe**
	Tastoxo	**3/Oxo**
	Tedoand	**1/Uta**
	Thotanf	**1/Paz**
	Tiarpax	**3/Lit**
	Toantom	**2/Asp**
	Tocarzi	**3/Tan**
	Todnaon	**2/Zid**
	Torzoxi	**1/Pop**
	Totocan	**3/Chr**
	Valgars	**3/Lil**

— Governors of Aethyrs (continued)	**Vastrim**	1/**Rii**
	Vavaamp	2/**Maz**
	Virooli	2/**Zom**
	Vivipos	2/**Uta**
	Vixpalg	3/**Asp**
	Usnarda	2/**Ich**
	Zafasai	2/**Zen**
	Zamfres	1/**Zid**
	Zaxanin	3/**Tor**
	Zildron	1/**Chr**
	Zirzird	3/**Maz**
great, greater — *see also* mighty	**drilpa, drilpi**	
Great Elemental Kings — *see* Elemental Kings		
groan	**holdo**	
grow strong	**ugeg, ugegi**	
guard	**bransg**	

H

half	**obza**
hand	**ozien, zien, ozol, zol**
handmaid — *see also* servant, minister	**qurlst**
happy	**ulcinin**
harbour (v.)	**blans**
harlot	**babalond**
harvest	**aziagiar**
have	**brin, brint, brints**
he (his, of him)	**tia, tox**
head	**dazis**
hearken	**solpeth, toatar**
heart	**monons**
heaven	**madriax, madriiax, peripsax, peripsol, piripsol, piripson**
— lower heavens	**oadriax**
hell-fire	**donasdogamatatastos**
her — *see* she	
here	**kures** (?)
herein	**emna**
Highest, The (name of God)	**Iaida**
hills	**ili-i** (AC: G)
holy	**ne; pire, pireda** (AC: VV)
Holy Ghost	**congamphlgh**

Holy Name (title of God)	**Idoian** (AC:VV)
Holy Names — *see* Divine and Holy Names	
Holy One	**Pir**
honor	**iaiadix**
house — *see also* dwelling-place, building, palace	**salman**
horn	**mospleh**
humility	**zuraah, zurah**
hundred	**eors**
hyacinth, hyacinthine	**avabh**
hyacinth pillars	**nazavabh**

I

I, me, my, myself	**ol**
in	**a, g, i; do** (AC: G)
in front of	**aspt**
include	**iaial**
increase	**coazior**
inhabit — *see also* be	**zodireda**
iniquity	**madrid**
intent (to the intent that)	**fafen**
invoke	**argedco** (?); **vinu** (AC: G)
is — *see* be	
it	**t**
itself	**zylna**

J

jaw **piadph**

joy **moz**

joy of God **mozod**

judgment **alca, balzizras**

Jupiter (associated angels and spirits):

- — Filia Lucis **Iana**
- — Filia Filiarum Lucis **Ized**
- — Filius Lucis **Dmal**
- — Filius Filiorum Lucis **Liba**
- — Seniors:
  - Air **Aaoxaif**
  - Earth **Aczinor**
  - Fire **Adoeoct**
  - Water **Saiinou**
- — King (of planetary hours) **Bynepor**
- — Princes (of planetary hours) **Baldago**, **Bartiro**, **Basmelo**, **Besgeme**, **Blingef**, **Butmono**
- — planetary angel **Zedekiel**

just **balit**

Just One, The (name of God) **Oiad**

justice **balt, baltim; padgze**

K

kingdom	**londoh, loadohi**
Kings (names of):	
— Elemental Kings:	
Air	**Tahaoeloj;**
	Bataivah (Senior)
Earth	**Thahaaotahe;**
	Iczhhcal (Senior)
Fire	**Ohooohaatan;**
	Edelprna (Senior)
Water	**Thahebyobeeatan;**
	Raagiosl (Senior)
— kings of planetary hours:	
Grand King	**Carmara**
Sol	**Bobogel**
Luna	**Blumaza**
Mars	**Babalel**
Mercury	**Bnaspol**
Jupiter	**Bynepor**
Venus	**Baligon**
Saturn	**Bnapsen**
— angelic kings	
— *see* angels	
know	**om, omax**
knowledge	**iadnah, iadnamad**
known	**ixomaxip**

L

laid up	**maasi**
lamentation	**eophan, ser**
lamp, lantern	**hubaio, hubar, hubaro**
law (make a law)	**ohorela**
legislate	**ohorela**
let there be — *see* be	
Life, Supreme (name of God)	**Iabes**
lift up — *see also* raise	**farzm, goholor;** **ofekufa** (AC: VV)
light	**olpirt**
likeness	**aziazor**
listen	**solpeth, toatar**
live (v.) — *see also* dwell	**apila**
live: He that Lives (name of God)	**Iadpil**
live: He that Lives Forever (name of God)	**Ioiad**
loins	**dax**
look about	**dorpha, dorphal**
Lord	**Enay, Na, Iabes**
Luna (associated angels and spirits:	
— Filia Lucis	**Me**
— Filia Filiarum Lucis	**Ab**
— Filius Lucis	**Ih**

— Filius Filiorum Lucis	**An**
— Seniors:	
Air	**Htmorda**
Earth	**Lzinopo**
Fire	**Asndood**
Water	**Laoaxrp**
— King (of planetary hours)	**Blumaza**
— Princes (of planetary hours)	**Bagledf**
	Baspalo
	Belmara
	Bragiop
	Bralges
	Brisfli
— planetary angel	**Levanael**

— *see also* moon

M

magnify, be magnified	**ovof**
make	**eol, ol**
make (made)	**oln; on** (AC: VV)
make a law	**ohorela**
make me/us (partakers)	**ozazm, ozazma**
man	**cordziz, molap, ollog, ollor, olora**
— works of man	**conisbra**
many (as many)	**plosi**
many (how many)	**irgil**
marble sleeves	**pidiai**
marrow	**tranan**
Mars (associated angels and spirits):	
— Filia Lucis	**Akele**
— Filia Filiarum Lucis	**Ekiei**
— Filius Lucis	**Heeoa**
— Filius Filiorum Lucis	**Rocle**
— Seniors:	
Air	**Habioro**
Earth	**Laidrom**
Fire	**Aaetpio**
Water	**Lsrahpm**
— King (of planetary hours)	**Babalel**
— Princes (of planetary hours)	**Bapnido**
	Befafes
	Binofom
	Bmilges
	Bminpol

	Busduna
— planetary angel	**Madimiel**
me	
— *see* I	
measure (v.)	**holq, maoffas**
member	**paombd**
memory	**papnor**
Mercury (associated angels and spirits):	
— Filia Lucis	**Azdobn**
— Filia Filiarum Lucis	**Madimi**
— Filius Lucis	**Beigia**
— Filius Filiorum Lucis	**Hagonel**
— Seniors:	
Air	**Avtotar**
Earth	**Acmbicu**
Fire	**Anodoin**
Water	**Soaixnt**
— King (of planetary hours)	**Bnaspol**
— Princes (of planetary hours)	**Barfort**
	Bazpama
	Bernole
	Blamapo
	Bliigan
	Blisdon
— planetary angel	**Corabiel**
mercy	**iehusoz, rit; okada** (AC:G)
midday	**bazm**
midst	**nothoa, zomd**
mighty	**canse, micalz, micalzo, micaolz, vohim**
— more mighty, mightier	**cruscanse, micalp**

— be mighty — *see also* great	**omicaolz**
mighty seat	**oxiayal**
millstone	**aviny**
mind (n.)	**manin**
mingle	**cynxir**
ministering angels	**Lang**
mix	**cynxir**
moment	**oanio**
moon — *see also* Luna	**graa**
moreover	**pilah**
moss	**mom**
Mother of All	**Exentaser** (AC:VV)
mother of vinegar	**lulo**
motion	**zna**
Mount of Olives (Mt. Olivet)	**adroch**
mouth	**butmon, butmona, butmoni**
mourning	**ser**
move	**zacam, zacar, zacare**
movement	**zna**
my, myself — *see* I	
mystery	**cicle, cicles**

N

name	**dooain, dooaip, dooiap, monasci, omaos**
names of angels — *see* angels	
names of cacodemons and demons — *see* demons	
names of God — *see* God — *see* Divine and Holy Names	
nest	**virq**
night	**dosig**
nine	**m, em**
no	**ag**
no one	**ag**
no place	**ripir**
noise — *see also* sound	**nidali**
none	**ag**
noon	**bazm**
nor	**larag, lu**
north	**lucal**
not	**ge, ip**
number (n.)	**cor, cormf, cormfa**
number (v.), numbered	**cormp, cormpo, cormpt**
numbers, Enochian — *see* Introduction, p.44	

O

o, oh	**c**
oak	**paeb**
obedience	**adna**
obey	**darbs**
of	**a, c, de**
olive	**quanis**
Olives, Mount of (Mt. Olivet)	**adroch**
on	**a, c**
one	**l, el, saga, gohed**
only	**crip, crp**
open (v.)	**odo**
or	**q**
our, ours — *see* we	
out of him	**geta**
over	**vors**

P

pair	**pala, pola**
palace	**poamal, poamalzod**
palm (of hand)	**nobloh**
part	**saanir**
peace	**etharzi**
perform	**fifis**
period	**capimao, capimaon**
philosopher's stone	**darr**
pillar	**naz**
pillar of gladness	**nazarth**
pillar of hyacinth	**nazavabh**
place (n.)	**pi**
— no place	**ripir**
place (v.)	**aala, oali**
planetary angels — *see* angels	
plant (v.)	**harg**
pleasure	**quasahi**
poison	**faboan**
pomp	**avavox**
possibility	**bab**
pour down	**panpir**
power	**bab, lansh, lonsa, lonshi, lonshin, micalz, micalzo, micaolz, nanaeel**

powerful	**micalz, micalzo, micaolz**
praise (n.)	**ecrin**
praise (v.)	**oecrimi, rest**
praising angels	**Luah**
praiseworthy	**akarinu** (AC: G)
pray	**lava**
precede	**tustax**
prepare	**abramg, abramig**
Princes (of planetary hours):	
Grand Prince	**Hagonel**
Sol	**Bablibo Bariges**
	Barnafa Bermale
	Bornogo Buscnab
Luna	**Bagledf Baspalo**
	Belmara Bragiop
	Bralges Brisfli
Mars	**Bapnido Befafes**
	Binofom Bmilges
	Bminpol Busduna
Mercury	**Barfort Bazpama**
	Bernole Bliigan
	Blisdon Blamapo
Jupiter	**Baldago Bartiro**
	Basmelo Besgeme
	Blingef Butmono
Venus	**Bagenol Benpagi**
	Binodab Bnagole
	Bormila Bonefom
Saturn	**Balceor Bamnode**
	Blintom Bmamgal
	Branglo Brorges
— *see also* Kings (of planetary hours)	
promise (n.)	**isro**

protect	**blans, bransg**
provide	**abraasa, tooat**
providence	**yarry**
put	**aala, oali**

Q

quality	**aspian**

R

raise	**farzm, goholor**
reasonable creature (man)	**cordziz**
rejoice	**chirlan**
regret	**moooah**
reign	**bogpa, sonf**
remain	**paaox, paaoxt**
remainder	**undl**
remembrance	**papnor**
repent	**moooah**
require	**unig**
rest (n.) (remainder)	**undl**
rest (v.)	**page**
rich	**las**
righteous	**balit, samvelg**
righteousness	**baltoh, piamol; Baeovib**
roar	**yor**
rock — *see also* stone	**patralx**
rod	**cab**
rotten	**qting**
rule	**bogpa, sonf**
Rulers of Aethyrs — *see* Governors of Aethyrs	
Rulers of Elements — *see* Divine and Holy Names	

S

saintly	**soyga**
— *see also* holy	
salt	**balye**
same	**lel**
Saturn (associated angels and spirits):	
— Filia Lucis	**Stimcul**
— Filia Filiarum Lucis	**Esemeli**
— Filius Lucis	**Stimcul**
— Filius Filiorum Lucis	**Ilemese**
— Seniors:	
Air	**Hipotga**
Earth	**Lhiansa**
Fire	**Arinnap**
Water	**Ligdisa**
— King (of planetary hours)	**Bnapsen**
— Princes (of planetary hours)	**Balceor**
	Bamnode
	Blintom
	Bmamgal
	Branglo
	Brorges
— planetary angel	**Sabathiel**
say	
— I say	**gohus**
— he says	**gohe, goho**
— we say	**gohia**
— saying	**gohol**
— is said (to you)	**gohulim**
— they have said (have spoken	**gohon**

scorpion	**siatris**
seal (n.)	**emetgis**
season	**capimao, nibm**
seat (n.) — *see also* set	**othil, thil, thild, thiln**
seat, mighty (throne)	**oxiayal**
second	**viu**
second time, for the — *see also* twice	**olaho** (AC:VV)
secret	**laiad**
see	**uran**
seething	**urelp**

Seniors of Elements (with planetary attributions):

	Air	Earth	Fire	Water
Sol	**Bataivah**	**Iczhhcal**	**Edelprna**	**Raagiosl**
Luna	**Htmorda**	**Lzinopo**	**Asndood**	**Laoaxrp**
Mars	**Habioro**	**Laidrom**	**Aaetpio**	**Lsrahpm**
Mercury	**Avtotar**	**Acmbicu**	**Anodoin**	**Soaixnt**
Jupiter	**Aaoxaif**	**Aczinor**	**Adoeoct**	**Saiinov**
Venus	**Ahaozpi**	**Alhctga**	**Aapdoce**	**Slgaiol**
Saturn	**Hipotga**	**Lhiansa**	**Arinnap**	**Ligdisa**

separate (v.) — *see also* divide	**tliob**
servant — *see also* handmaid, minister, serve, steward	**noco, noquod, noquodi, noquol**
serve	**aboapri**
set (v.)	**othil**
settle	**alar**

she	**pi**
— her, of her	**tilb, tlb, tiobl**
shelter	**blans**
shine	**loholo**
show oneself	**zamran**
shrine	**arba** (AC:VV)
sickle	**puim**
sin (v.)	**doalim**
sing praises	**oecrimi**
sink	**carbaf**
sit	**trint**
six	**norz**
skirt (n.)	**unalab**
sleeve	**collal, pidiai**
slimy things made of dust	**apachama**
smile (?)	**ucim**
Sol (associated angels and spirits):	
— Filia Lucis	**El (L)**
— Filia Filiarum Lucis	**S**
— Filius Lucis	**I**
— Filius Filiorum Lucis	**E**
— Seniors:	
Air	**Bataivah**
Earth	**Iczhhcal**
Fire	**Edelprna**
Water	**Raagiosl**
— King (of planetary hours)	**Bobogel**
— Princes (of planetary hours)	**Bablibo**

	Bariges
	Barnafa
	Bermale
	Bornogo
	Buscnab
— planetary angel	**Semeliel**
— *see also* sun	
so that	**ar**
son	**nor, noromi**
sorrow	**tibibp**
sound	**sapah**
— *see also* noise	
south	**babage, babagen**
speak	**camliax**
— *see also* say	
speech from God	**loagaeth, logaeth, logaah, logah**
spirit	**gah**
spirit (of man)	**congamphlgh**
Spirit of Air (Tablet of Union)	**Exarp**
Spirit of Earth (Tablet of Union)	**Nanta**
Spirit of Fire (Tablet of Union)	**Bitom**
Spirit of Water (Tablet of Union)	**Hcoma**
spirits, names of	
— *see* angels, demons	
stand	**biah**
star	**aoiveae**

steward — *see also* handmaid, minister, servant	**balzarg**
sting	**grosb**
stir up	**lring**
stone — *see also* rock	**orri**
stone, philospher's	**darr**
stooping	**abai**
stranger	**gosaa**
strength — *see also* strong	**ugear, umplif**
stretch forth (?)	**zil**
Stretch-Forth-and-Conquer (name of God)	**Zilodarp**
strong (grow strong)	**ugeg, ugegi**
strong (stronger) — *see also* mighty	**givi**
successively	**capimali**
such	**cors**
sulphur	**salbrox; dlasod** (alchemical)
sun — *see also* Sol	**ror**
Supreme Life (name of God)	**Iabes**
surge (n.)	**molvi**
swear (swore, sworn)	**surzas, znurza, zurza**
sword	**napta, napeai, nazpsad**

T

talk	**brita**
— *see also* speak, say	
tartar	**lulo**
tell them	**mapsama**
temple	**siaion**
that (so that)	**fafen; na** (AC: VV)
— which	**ar, ds**
the	**a**
thee	
— *see* thou	
them	
— *see* they	
there	**da**
therefore	**ca**
these	**unal**
— *see also* this, those	
they, them	**par, z**
third	
— *see* three	
this	**oi**
— *see also* these, those	
thorn	**nanba**
those	**priaz, priazi**
— *see also* this, these	
thou	**ils**
— thee	**yls; ta** (AC: G)
— thy	**il, q**
— *see also* you	

thought	**angelard**
thousand	**matb**
three, third	**d**
throne	**oxiayal**
thunder	**avavago, const, coraxo**
thy — *see* thou	
time	**capimao, cocasb, cocasg**
time after time	**capimali, capmiali**
to	**de**
torment	**mir**
tower	**umadea**
treasure	**limlal**
Trinity	**Na**
triumph (v.)	**homtoh**
truss (v.)	**commah**
truth	**vaoan; vooan** (with fallen angels)
twelve	**os**
twenty-fourth (part)	**ol**
twice — *see also* two, second	**olani**
two (separated)	**pala**
two (together) — *see also* second, twice	**pola**

U

under, underneath	**oroch, orocha**
understand — *see also* know	**om**
understanding — *see also* knowledge, wisdom	**oma**
unspeakable	**adphaht**
until	**cacrg**
unto	**pambt, pugo**
upon	**mirc**
us — *see* we	

V

van (v.) (winnow)	**ar**
variety	**damploz**
veil	**zodimibe** (AC:G)
Venus (associated angels and spirits):	
— Filia Lucis	**Ese**
— Filia Filiarum Lucis	**Ath**
— Filius Lucis	**Ilr**
— Filius Filiorum Lucis	**Ave**
— Seniors:	
Air	**Ahaozpi**
Earth	**Alhctga**
Fire	**Aapdoce**
Water	**Slgaiol**
— King (of planetary hours)	**Baligon**
— Princes (of planetary hours)	**Benpagi** **Binodab** **Bnagole** **Bonefom** **Bormila** **Busduna**
— planetary angel	**Nogahel**
vessel (container)	**izizop, zizop**
vestures — *see also* garments	**zimz**
vex	**dodpal, dodrmni, dods**
vexation	**dodsih**
vial	**efafafe, ofafafe**
vinegar, mother of	**lulo**

virgin	**paradiz**
visit	**f, ef, t**
voice	**bia, bial, bien, faaip**
vomit	**oxex**

W

walk	**insi**
want	**gil** (?)
warden (of the Aethyr *Bag*)	**Lixipsp** (AC: VV)
was — *see* be	
water (v.)	**zlida**
water (n.)	**zodinu** (AC: G)
Water (Element):	
— Spirit	**Hcoma**
— Holy Names ruling:	**Mph Arsl Gaiol**
— Divine Names ruling sub-elements:	
Air of Water	**Obgota Aabco**
Earth of Water	**Maladi Olaad**
Fire of Water	**Iaaasd Atapa**
Water of Water	**Nelapr Omebb**
— Demonic Names ruling sub-elements:	
Air of Water	**Atogbo Ocbaa**
Earth of Water	**Idalam Daalo**
Fire of Water	**Dsaaai Apata**
Water of Water	**Rpalen Bbemo**
— Seniors (with planetary associations):	
Sol (Elemental King)	**Raagiosl**
Luna	**Laoaxrp**
Mars	**Lsrahpm**
Mercury	**Soaixnt**
Jupiter	**Saiinov**
Venus	**Slgaiol**
Saturn	**Ligdisa**
— Great Elemental King	**Thahebyobeeatan**

wax strong	**ugeg, ugegi**
we, our, us	**ge**
— in ours	**helech**
weave	**oado**
weed out	**fifalz**
weeping	**raclir**
were	
— *see* be	
west	**sobol**
wherefore	**darsar**
wherein	**quiin; vo** (AC:VV)
which	**ds**
— *see also* who	
while (n.)	**capimao**
who	**ds**
— whom	**casarm, casarma, casarmg, casarmi, sobam**
— whose	**casarman, soba, sobca, sobha, sobol, sobra, soha**
whole	**saga**
why	**bagle, baglen**
wicked	**babalon**
will of God	**soyga, aldaraia**
will (your will be done)	**gemeganza**
wind	**ozongon, zong**
window	**como**
wine	**roxtan**
wing	**upaah**
winnow	**ar**

wisdom — *see also* knowledge, understanding	**ananael, miketh**
with	**a, c**
woe	**ohio**
wonder (n.)	**sald, zirn**
work (v.)	**vaul, vaun**
workman	**canal**
works of man	**conisbra**
wormwood	**tatan**
worship	**boaluahe** (AC: G)
worshipper	**hoath**
wrath	**unph, vonph, vonpho**

Y

yea	**noib**
you	**g, gi, nonci**
— to you	**nonca, noncf, noncp**
— your	**g**
— yourselves	**amiran**
— *see also* thou	

End of English-Angelic Dictionary

THE ENOCHIAN CALLS

This edited version of the Enochian Calls follows closely Dee's fair copy in the manuscript of the *48 Claves Angelicae* (Cracow, 13 April-13 July 1584). I have modernised his often erratic spelling, punctuation, and word-division; and here and there I have replaced an archaic word or phrase with its modern equivalent. Other minor amendments have been made to allow the English text to be compared with the Enochian more closely. I have, however, resisted the temptation to interfere with the Enochian text, except for corrections which Dee himself made. Capitalisation and word-division conform to the English text, in accord with my grammatical analysis of Enochian. The Enochian words appear directly under the English words to which they most closely relate, except in a few instances where either the English text or the Enochian text is defective. There is still room for dispute in some of the identifications, and in one or two instances arbitrary decisions had to be made. Further information on the exact shades of meaning, as far as can be determined, will be found in the dictionary section.

The First Call

I reign over you, says the God of Justice, in power exalted
Ol sonf vors g, gohó Iad Balt, lansh

above the firmaments of wrath; in Whose hands the sun is as a
calz vonpho; Sobra zol ror i ta

sword, and the moon as a penetrating fire; Who measures your
nazpsad, graa ta malprg; Ds holq

garments in the midst of my vestures, and trussed you together
qaa nothoa zimz, od commah

as the palms of my hands; Whose seats I garnished with the
ta nobloh zien; Soba thil gnonp

fire of gathering; Who beautified your garments with admiration;
prge aldi; Ds urbs oboleh g rsam;

to Whom I made a law to govern the Holy Ones; Who delivered
Casarm ohorela taba Pir; Ds zonrensg

you a rod with the ark of knowledge. Moreover, you lifted up your
cab erm iadnah. Pilah farzm

voices and swore obedience and faith to Him that lives, and who
znurza adna gono Iadpil, ds

triumphs; Whose beginning is not, nor end cannot be; Who
homtoh; Soba ipam, lu ipamis; Ds

shines as a flame in the midst of your palace, and reigns amongst
loholo vep zomd poamal, od bogpa aai

you as the balance of righteousness and truth. Move, therefore,
ta piap piamol od vooan. Zacare, ca,

and show yourselves; open the mysteries of your creation; be
od zamran; odo cicle qaa;

friendly unto me; for I am the servant of the same God as you,
zorge, lap zirdo noco Mad,

the true worshipper of the Highest.
hoath Iaida.

The Second Call

Can the wings of the winds understand your voices of wonder,
Adgt upaah zong om faaip sald,

o you the second of the First? Whom the burning flames have
viu L? Sobam ialprg

framed within the depth of my jaws; Whom I have prepared
izazaz piadph; Casarma abramg

as cups for a wedding, or as the flowers in their beauty
ta talho paracleda, q ta lorlsq turbs

for the chamber of righteousness. Stronger are your feet than
ooge baltoh. Givi chis lusd

the barren stone, and mightier are your voices than the manifold
orri, od micalp chis bia

winds; for you are become a building such as is not, but in
ozongon; lap noan trof cors ta ge, oq

the mind of the All-Powerful. Arise, says the First; move,
manin Iaidon. Torzu, gohe L; zacar,

therefore, unto his servants; show yourselves in power, and
ca, c noqod; zamran micalzo, od

make me a strong seething; for I am of Him that lives forever.
ozazm urelp; lap zir Ioiad.

The Third Call

Behold, says your God, I am a circle on whose hands stand
Micma, goho Piad, zir comselh a zien biah

twelve kingdoms. Six are the seats of living breath, the
os londoh. Norz chis othil gigipah,

rest are as sharp sickles, or the horns of death, wherein
undl chis ta puim, q mospleh teloch, quiin

the creatures of the earth are and are not, except by my
toltorg chisi chis ge, m

own hands, which also sleep and shall rise. In the first I made you
ozien, ds t brgda od torzul. I li eol

stewards, and placed you in seats twelve of government, giving
balzarg, od aala thiln os netaab, dluga

unto every one of you power successively over 456, the true
vomsarg lonsa capmiali vors cla,

ages of time, to the intent that, from the highest vessels and
homil cocasb, fafen izizop od

the corners of your governments, you might work my power,
miinoag de g netaab, vaun nanaeel,

pouring down the fires of life and increase on the earth
panpir malpirgi caosg

continually. Thus you are become the skirts of justice and truth.
pild. Noan unalah balt od vooan.

In the name of the same, your God, lift up, I say, yourselves.
Dooiap Mad, goholor, gohus, amiran.

Behold His mercies flourish, and His Name is become mighty
Micma iehusoz cacacom, od dooain noar micaolz

amongst us; in Whom we say: Move, descend, and apply
aai om; Casarmg gohia: Zacar, uniglag, od imvamar

yourselves unto us, as unto the partakers of the secret wisdom
pugo plapli ananael

of your Creation.
qaan.

The Fourth Call

I have set my feet in the south, and have looked about me,
Othil lasdi babage, od dorpha,

saying: are not the thunders of increase numbered 33,
gohol: g chis ge avavago cormp pd,

which reign in the second angle? Under whom I have placed
ds sonf viu diu? Casarmi oali

9639, whom none has yet numbered but one, in whom the second
mapm, sobam ag cormpo crp l, casarmg

beginning of things are and wax strong; which also success-
croodzi chis od ugeg; ds t, capimali,

ively, are the number of time; and their powers are as the
chis capimaon; od lonshin chis ta

first 456. Arise, you sons of pleasure, and visit the earth for
lo cla. Torgu, nor quasahi, od f caosga; bagle

I am the Lord your God, which is and lives. In the name of the
zir enay Iad, ds i od apila. Dooaip

Creator, move, and show yourselves as pleasant deliverers,
Qaal, zacar, od zamran obelisong,

that you may praise him amongst the sons of men.
rest el aaf nor molap.

The Fifth Call

The mighty sounds have entered in the third angle, and are
Sapah zimii d diu, od

become as olives on the Mount of Olives, looking with gladness
noas ta quanis Adroch, dorphal

upon the earth, and dwelling in the brightness of the heavens as
caosg, od faonts piripsol ta

comforters; unto whom I fastened pillars of gladness nineteen,
blior; casarm amipzi naz arth af,

and gave them vessels to water the earth with [all] her creatures;
od dlugar zizop zlida caosgi tol torgi;

and they are the brothers of the first and second, and the
od z chis esiasch l ta viu, od

beginning of their own seats, which are garnished with continual
iaod thild, ds

burning lamps 69636, whose numbers are as the first, the ends
hubar peoal, soba cormfa chis ta la, uls

and the content of time. Therefore come and obey your
od q cocasb. Ca niis od darbs

creation; visit us in peace and comfort; include us as receivers
qaas; f etharzi od bliora; iaial ednas

of your mysteries, because our Lord and Master is all One.
cicles, bagle ge Iad L.

The Sixth Call

The spirits of the fourth angle are nine, mighty in the firmament
Gah s diu em, micalzo pilzin;

of waters; whom the first has planted as a torment to the
sobam el harg mir

wicked and a garland to the righteous, giving unto them
babalon od obloc samvelg, dlugar

fiery darts to winnow the earth, and 7699 continual workmen;
malprg ar caosgi, od acam canal;

whose courses visit with comfort the earth, and are in govern-
sobol zar f bliard caosgi, od chis a netab

ment and continuance as the second and third. Wherefore harken
od miam ta viu od d. Darsar solpeth

unto my voice; I have talked of you, and I move you in power
bien; brita od zacam g micalzo

and presence, you whose works shall be a song of honour and the
sobha ath trian luiahe od

praise of your God in your creation.
ecrin Mad qaaon.

The Seventh Call

The east is a house of virgins, singing praises amongst the
Raas i salman paradiz, oecrimi aao

flames of first glory, wherein the Lord has opened his mouth,
ialpirgah, quiin Enay butmon,

and they are become 28 living dwellings, in whom the strength
od i noas ni paradial, casarmg ugear

of man rejoices; and they are apparelled with ornaments of
chirlan; od zonac

brightness, such as work wonders on all creatures; whose
luciftian, cors ta vaul zirn tol hami; soba

kingdoms and continuance are as the third and fourth, strong
londoh od miam chis ta d od es,

towers and places of comfort, the seats of mercy and continu-
umadea od pi bliar, othil rit od miam.

ance. O you servants of mercy, move, appear, sing praises
C noquol rit, zacar, zamran, oecrimi

unto the Creator; and be mighty amongst us; for to this
Qadah; od omicaolz aai om; bagle

remembrance is given power, and our strength waxes
papnor i dlugam lonshi, od umplif ugegi

strong in our comforter.
bigliad.

The Eighth Call

The midday, the first, is as the third heaven made of pillars
Bazm, elo, i ta piripson oln naz

of hyacinth 26, in whom the elders are become strong;
avabh ox, casarmg uran chis ugeg;

which I have prepared for my own righteousness, says the Lord;
ds abramig baltoha, goho Iad;

whose long continuance shall be as bucklers to the stooping
soba mian trian ta lolcis abai

dragon, and like unto the harvest of a widow. How many are
vovin, od aziagiar rior. Irgil chis

there which remain in the glory of the earth, which are, and
da ds paaox busd caosgo, ds chis, od

shall not see death until this house fall, and the dragon
ip uran teloah cacrg oi salman loncho, od vovina

sink! Come away, for the thunders have spoken; come away,
carbaf! Niiso, bagle avavago gohon; niiso,

for the crowns of the temple, and the coat of Him that is,
bagle momao siaion, od mabza Iado i,

was, and shall be crowned, are divided. Come, appear to the
as, momar, poilp. Niis, zamran

terror of the earth, and to our comfort, and of such as
ciaofi caosgo, od bliors, od cors i ta

are prepared.
abramig.

The Ninth Call

A mighty guard of fire, with two-edged swords flaming (which
Micaolz bransg prgel, napta ialpor (ds

have vials eight of wrath for two times and a half, whose
brin efafafe p vonpho olani od obza, sobca

wings are of wormwood, and of the marrow of salt), have settled
upaah chis tatan, od tranan balye) alar

their feet in the west, and were measured with their ministers
lusda sobol, od chis holq c noquodi

9996. These gather up the moss of the earth as the rich man
cial. Unal aldon mom caosgo ta las ollor

does his treasure. Cursed are they whose iniquities they are!
gnay limlal. Amma chiis sobca madrid z chis!

In their eyes are millstones greater than the earth, and
Ooanoan chis aviny drilpi caosgin, od

from their mouths rain seas of blood: their heads are covered
butmoni parm zumvi cnila: daziz ethamz

with diamonds, and upon their hands are marble sleeves. Happy
a childao, od mirc ozol chi pidiai collal. Ulcinin

is he on whom they frown not, because the God of Righteousness
a sobam ucim, bagle Iad Baltoh

rejoices in them. Come away (and not your vials)! For
chirlan par. Niiso (od ip ofafafe)! Bagle

the time is such as requires comfort.
a cocasb i cors ca unig blior.

The Tenth Call

The thunders of judgment and wrath are numbered and are
Coraxo chis cormp od

harboured in the north in the likeness of an oak, whose
blans lucal aziazior paeb, soba

branches are nests 22 of lamentation and weeping laid up
lilonon chis virq op eophan od raclir maasi

for the earth, which burn night and day, and vomit out
bagle caosgi, ds ialpon dosig od basgim, od oxex

the heads of scorpions, and live sulphur mingled with poison.
dazis siatris, od salbrox cynxir faboan.

These are the thunders that 5678 times in the 24th part
Unal chis const ds daox cocasg ol

of a moment roar with a hundred mighty earthquakes, and a
oanio yor eors vohim gizyax, od

thousand times as many surges, which rest not, nor know
matb cocasg plosi molvi, ds page ip, larag om

any echoing time. Here one rock brings forth a
droln matorb cocasb. Emna l patralx yolci

thousand, even as the heart of man does his thoughts.
matb, nomig monons olora gnay angelard.

Woe Woe Woe Woe Woe Woe, yes, Woe be to the earth, for
Ohio Ohio Ohio Ohio Ohio Ohio, noib, Ohio caosgon, bagle

her iniquity is, was, and shall be great. Come away — but not
madrid i, zirop, chiso drilpa. Niiso - crip ip

your noises.
nidali.

The Eleventh Call

The mighty seat groaned and there were five thunders
Oxiayal holdo od zirom o coraxo

which flew into the east, and the Eagle spake and cried
ds zildar raasy, od vabzir camliax od bahal:

with a loud voice: Come away! And they gathered themselves
Niiso!

together and became the house of death; of whom it is measured,
salman teloch; casarman holq,

and it is as they are whose number is 31. Come away! For
od t i ta z chis soba cormf i ga. Niisa! Bagle

I prepare for you. Move, therefore, and show yourselves;
abramg noncp. Zacare, ca, od zamran;

open the mysteries of your creation; be friendly unto me, for
odo cicle qaa; zorge, lap

I am the servant of the same God as you, the true worshipper
zirdo noco Mad, hoath

of the Highest.
Iaida.

The Twelfth Call

O you that reign in the south, and are 28, the lanterns
Nonci ds sonf babage, od chis ob, hubaio

of sorrow bind up your girdles, and visit us! Bring down
tibibp allar atraah, od ef! Drix

your followers 3663, that the Lord may be magnified, Whose
fafen mian, ar Enay ovof, Soba

name amongst you is Wrath. Move, I say, and show
dooain aai i Vonph. Zacar, gohus, od zamran;

yourselves; open the mysteries of your creation; be friendly
odo cicle qaa; zorge

unto me, for I am the servant of the same God as you, the true
lap zirdo noco Mad,

worshipper of the Highest.
hoath Iaida.

The Thirteenth Call

O you swords of the south, which have 42 eyes to stir up
Napeai babagen, ds brin vx ooaona lring

the wrath of sin, making men drunken which are empty;
vonph doalim, eolis ollog orsba ds chis affa;

behold the promise of God, and the power of Him, which is
micma isro Mad, od lonshi Tox, ds i

called amongst you a bitter sting; move and show yourselves;
umd aai grosb; zacar od zamran;

open the mysteries of your creation; be friendly unto me,
odo cicle qaa; zorge,

for I am the servant of the same God as you, the true
lap zirdo noco Mad,

worshipper of the Highest.
hoath Iaida.

The Fourteenth Call

O you sons of fury, the daughters of the Just, which sit
Noromi bagie, pasbs Oiad, ds trint

upon 24 seats, vexing all creatures of the earth with age;
mirc ol thil, dods tol ham caosgo homin;

which have under you 1636; behold the voice of God, the
ds brin oroch quar; micma bial Oiad, a

promise of Him, which is called amongst you extreme justice;
isro Tox, ds i um aai Baltim;

move and show yourselves; open the mysteries of your creation;
zacar od zamran; odo cicle qaa;

be friendly unto me, for I am the servant of the same God as you,
zorge, lap zirdo noco Mad,

the true worshipper of the Highest.
hoath Iaida.

The Fifteenth Call

O thou the governor of the first flame, under whose
Ils tabaan l ialprt, casarman

wings are 6379, which weave the earth with dryness,
upaahi chis darg, ds oado caosgi orscor,

who knowest the great name Righteousness and the seal
ds omax monasci Baeovib od emetgis

of honour: move and show yourselves; open the mysteries
iaiadix: zacar od zamran; odo cicle

of your creation; be friendly unto me, for I am the servant
qaa; zorge, lap zirdo noco

of the same God as you, the true worshipper of the Highest.
Mad, hoath Iaida.

The Sixteenth Call

O thou second flame, the house of justice, who hast thy
Ils viu ialprt salman balt, ds

beginning in glory, and shall comfort the just; who walkest
acroodzi busd, od bliorax balit; ds insi

on the earth with feet 8763 that understand and separate
caosg lusdan emod ds om od tliob:

creatures: great art thou in the God of Stretch-forth-and-
drilpa geh ils Mad Zilodarp.

Conquer. Move and show yourselves; open the mysteries of
Zacar od zamran; odo cicle

your creation; be friendly unto me, for I am the servant of the
qaa; zorge, lap zirdo noco

same God as you, the true worshipper of the Highest.
Mad, hoath Iaida.

The Seventeenth Call

O thou third flame, whose wings are thorns to stir up vexation,
Ils d ialprt, soba upaah chis nanba zixlay dodsih,

and who hast 7336 living lamps going before thee, whose God
od brint taxs hubaro tustax ylsi, soba Iad

is wrath in anger: gird up the loins of thee and harken. Move and
i vonpo unph: aldon dax il od toatar. Zacar od

show yourselves; open the mysteries of your creation; be friendly
zamran; odo cicle qaa; zorge,

unto me, for I am the servant of the same God as you, the true
lap zirdo noco Mad,

worshipper of the Highest.
hoath Iaida.

The Eighteenth Call

O thou mighty light and burning flame of comfort, which
Ils micaolz olpirt ialprg bliors, ds

openest the glory of God to the centre of the earth; in whom the
odo busdir Oiad ovoars caosgo; casarmg

secrets of truth 6332 have their abiding; which is called in thy
laïad eran brints cafafam; ds i umd a q

kingdom Joy, and not to be measured: be thou a window of
loadohi Moz, od maoffas: bolp como

comfort unto me. Move and show yourselves; open the
bliort pambt. Zacar od zamran; odo

mysteries of your creation; be friendly unto me, for I am the
cicle qaa; zorge, lap zirdo

servant of the same God as you, the true worshipper of the
noco Mad, hoath

Highest.
Iaida.

The Call of the Thirty Aethyrs

O you heavens which dwell in the (first Air), which are
Madriax ds praf (LIL), chis

mighty in the parts of the earth, and which execute the
micaolz saanir caosgo, od fifis

judgment of the Highest! To you it is said: Behold the
balzizras Iaida!. Nonca gohulim: Micma

face of your God, the beginning of comfort, Whose eyes are
adoian Mad, iaod bliorb, Soba ooaona chis

the brightness of heavens; Who provided you for the govern-
luciftias peripsol; Ds abraasa noncf netaaib

ment of the earth, and her unspeakable variety, furnishing
caosgi, od tilb adphaht damploz, tooat

you with a power of understanding, to dispose all things
noncf g micalz oma, lrasd tofglo

according to the providence of Him that sits on the Holy Throne;
marb yarry Idoigo;

and Who rose up in the beginning, saying: the earth, let her
od torzulp iaodaf, gohul: caosga,

be governed by her parts, and let there be division in
tabaord saanir, od christeos yrpoil

her, that the glory of her may be always drunken and vexed in
tiobl, busdir tilb noaln paid orsba od dodrmni

itself. The course of her, let it run with the heavens, and as a
zylna. Elzap tilb, parm gi peripsax, od ta

handmaid let her serve them. One season, let it confound
qurlst booapis. L nibm, oucho

another; and let there be no creature upon or within her
symp; od christeos ag toltorn mirc q tiobl

the same. All her members, let them differ in their qualities; and
lel. Ton paombd, dilzmo aspian; od

let there be no one creature equal with another. The
christeos ag l tortorn parach a symp.

reasonable creatures of the earth, let them vex and weed out
Cordziz, dodpal od fifalz

one another; and the dwelling places, let them forget their
l smnad; od fargt, bams

names. The works of man and his pomp, let them be defaced.
omaoas. Conisbra od avavox, tonug.

The buildings of her, let them become caves for the beasts of the
Orsca tbl, noasmi tabges levithmong;

field; confound the understanding of her with darkness. Why?
unchi omp tilb ors. Bagle?

I regret that I made man. One while let her be known, and
Moooah ol cordziz. L capimao ixomaxip, od

another while a stranger; because she is the bed of a harlot,
ca cocasb gosaa; baglen pi tianta a babalond,

and the dwelling place of him-that-is-fallen. O you heavens,
od faorgt teloc vovim. Madriiax,

arise! The lower heavens underneath you, let them serve you.
torzu! Oadriax orocha, aboapri.

Govern those that govern; cast down such as fall; bring forth
Tabaori priaz ar tabas; adrpan cors ta dobix; yolcam

with those that increase, and destroy the rotten. No place let it
priazi ar coazior, od quasb qting. Ripir

remain in one number; add and diminish, until the stars be
paaoxt saga cor; uml od prdzar, cacrg aoiveae

numbered. Arise, move, and appear before the covenant of His
cormpt. Torzu, zacar, od zamran aspt sibsi

mouth, which He has sworn unto us in His justice; open the
butmona, ds surzas Tia baltan; odo

mysteries of your creation, and make us partakers of undefiled
cicle qaa, od ozazma plapli

knowledge.
iadnamad.

BIBLIOGRAPHY

Further reading on Dee, Kelley, and the Enochian Language:

Manuscripts

London:

Appendix MS XLVI, parts 1 and 2. Manuscript of Dee's 'Spiritual Diaries' edited by Meric Casaubon.

Sloane MS 78, art.11. Part of Dee's 'Liber mysteriorum sextus et sanctus'.

Sloane MS 3188. Dee's 'Spiritual Diaries' from 22 December 1581 to 30 May 1583.

Sloane MS 3189. Dee's 'Liber mysteriorum sextus et sanctus' in Edward Kelley's handwriting.

Sloane MS 3191, arts.1-4. 'Claves angelicae'; 'Liber scientia auxilii et victoria terrestris'; 'De heptarchia mystica'; Tabula bonorum angelorum invocationes'.

Sloane MS 3677. Elias Ashmole's copy of Dee's 'Spiritual Diaries'.

Sloane MS 3678, art.1. Elias Ashmole's copy of Sloane MS 3191.

Warburg MS FBH 510. John Dee's 'Tuba veneris'.

Cambridge:

Trinity College MS O. 4. 20. Dee's list of his books made on 6 September 1583.

Oxford:

Ashmole MS 422, art.2. Notes copied by Elias Ashmole from Dee's fifth 'Liber mysteriorum'.

Ashmole MS 1790, I-IV. 'Praefatio Latina in actionem'; a collection of papers relating to Dee's actions with the spirits; Elias Ashmole's observations and collections concerning the same; Elias Ashmole's correspondence relating to Dee.

Rawlinson MS 923, arts.A.12; B.10. An account of John Dee's family and notes on Meric Casaubon's edition of the 'Spiritual Diaries'.

Printed Editions of Dee's Works

Autobiographical Tracts of Dr John Dee, Warden of the College of Manchester, ed. James Crossley. *Chetham Society Publications,* Vol.XXIV. Manchester, 1851.

Diary for the years 1595-1601, ed. John E Bailey. Privately printed, 1880.

Monas Hieroglyphica. Antwerp, 1564, reprinted Frankfurt, 1591.

Hieroglyphic Monad, tr. J W Hamilton-Jones, London, 1947.

Monas Hieroglyphica, tr. C H Josten, *AMBIX,* XII (1964), 84-221.

Private Diary, ed. James O Halliwell. *Camden Society Publications,* Vol.XIX. London, 1842.

A True & Faithful Relation of what passed for many Yeers Between Dr John Dee... and Some Spirits, ed. Meric Casaubon. London, 1659. Casaubon's own copy with his handwritten corrections is in the Bodleian Library, shelf mark D. 8. 14 art, while a copy in the British Museum contains revealing marginal notes by contemporaries of Casaubon's, shelf mark 719. m. 12. Reprinted Askin Publishers, London, 1974.

Printed Sources

Agrippa, Henry Cornelius. *Three Books of Occult Philosophy,* tr. J(ames) F(rench). London, 1651. Reprinting Askin Publishers, London, 1979.

Bailey, John E. 'Dee and Trithemius's "Steganography"', *N&Q,* 5th series, XI (1879), 401-2, 422-3.

Crowley, Aleister. 'Liber XXX AERUM vel Saeculi sub figura CCCCXVIII being of the Angels of the Thirty Aethyrs, the Vision and the Voice'. *The Equinox* I.5, supplement, 1911. Republished as *The Vision and the Voice* ed. Israel Regardie, Dallas, 1972.

Crowley, Aleister. 'Liber LXXXIV vel Chanokh: a brief abstract of the Symbolic Representation of the Universe derived by Doctor John Dee through the scrying of Sir Edward Kelly'. *The Equinox* I. 7: 229-243, 1912; I. 8: 99-128, 1912.

Dalton, Ormonde M. 'Notes on Wax Discs used by Dr Dee', *Proceedings of the Society of Antiquaries of London,* XXI (1906-7), 380-3.

Deacon, Richard. *John Dee: Scientist, Geographer, Astrologer and Secret Agent to Elizabeth I.* London, 1968.

French, Peter J. *John Dee: The World of an Elizabethan Magus.* London, 1972. Contains a very full Dee bibliography.

Hay, G, Wilson, C, Turner, R and Langford, D. *The Necronomicon,* London, 1978.

Hooke, Robert. *The Posthumous Works.* London, 1705.

Hort, Gertrude M. *Dr John Dee: Elizabethan Mystic and Astrologer.* London, 1922.

Josten, C H. 'An Unknown Chapter in the Life of John Dee', in *JWCI,* XXVIII (1965), 223-57.

King, Francis. *Ritual Magic in England.* London, 1970.

La Vey, Anton Szandor. *The Satanic Bible.* Secaucus, 1969.

Laycock, Donald. 'How to Speak the Angelical Language', *Arc* 3, 19-21, London, 1973.

Mathers, S L MacGregor and Crowley, Aleister. *The Book of the Goetia of Solomon the King.* London, 1904.

McCulloch, S C. 'John Dee: Elizabethan Doctor of Science and Magic', *South Atlantic Quarterly,* L (1951), 72-85.

Prideaux, W R B. 'Books from John Dee's Library', *N&Q,* 9th series, VIII (1901), 137-8.

Prideaux, W R B. 'Books from John Dee's Library', *N&Q,* VIII (1904), 241.

Regardie, Francis Israel, ed. *The Golden Dawn,* 4 vols., 1937-1940. Minnesota, 1971.

Skinner, Stephen. 'The Magic of John Dee', *Cosmos* 1 (12).1, 12-13, 1974.

Skinner, Stephen. *Enochian Magic.* NYP

Smith, Charlotte Fell. *John Dee: 1527-1608.* London, 1909.

Smith, Thomas. *Vita Joannis Dee,* in *Vitae quorundam eruditissimorum et illustrium virorum.* London, 1707.

Smith, Thomas. *The Life of John Dee,* tr. William A Ayton. London, 1908.

Tait, Hugh. '"The Devil's Looking Glass": The Magical Speculum of Dr John Dee', *Horace Walpole: Writer, Politician, and*

Connoisseur, ed Warren Hunting Smith. New Haven and London, 1967.
Trithemius, Johannes. *Steganographia.* Frankfurt, 1606.
Vinci, Leo. *Gmicalzoma!* London and New York, 1976.
Yates, Frances A. *Giordano Bruno and the Hermetic Tradition.* London and Chicago, 1964.
Yates, Frances A. *The Rosicrucian Enlightenment.* London, 1972.

DR JOHN DEE'S SPIRITUAL DIARIES (1583–1608)

being a reset and fully corrected edition of the reception of the Enochian language in *A True & Faithful Relation . . .* now *with all the Latin passages translated (no other edition has the Latin translated).*

Edited by Dr Stephen Skinner

- ISBN: 978-1912212-13-2 (cloth)
- Price: £76.00 / $96.00 (cloth)
- Pages: 844
- Illustrations: 26 plus 6 in full colour
- Published: 2019

This is a completely revamped and corrected edition of *A True & Faithful Relation of what passed between Dr. John Dee . . . and some Spirits*, printed by Meric Casaubon in 1659. Now re-edited by Dr Stephen Skinner, from the original manuscripts in the British Library, correcting over 1,000 errors, with an introduction, appendices, footnotes, supplementary texts, additional illustrations, and a Dee timeline. Corrections are included from the original notes of Meric Casaubon, Elias Ashmole and William Shippen. Sections which were originally missing from Casaubon's edition have been added. Angels, spirits, people, places, dates and times have been fully footnoted and listed, and Casaubon's errors corrected.

TO OUR READERS

Weiser Books, an imprint of Red Wheel/Weiser, publishes books across the entire spectrum of occult, esoteric, speculative, and New Age subjects. Our mission is to publish quality books that will make a difference in people's lives without advocating any one particular path or field of study. We value the integrity, originality, and depth of knowledge of our authors.

Our readers are our most important resource, and we appreciate your input, suggestions, and ideas about what you would like to see published.

Visit our website at *www.redwheelweiser.com,* where you can learn about our upcoming books and free downloads, and also find links to sign up for our newsletter and exclusive offers.
You can also contact us at info@rwwbooks.com or at

Red Wheel/Weiser, LLC
65 Parker Street, Suite 7
Newburyport, MA 01950